Toolkit for Water Policies and Governance

CONVERGING TOWARDS THE OECD COUNCIL RECOMMENDATION ON WATER

OECD
BETTER POLICIES FOR BETTER LIVES

Please cite this publication as:
OECD (2021), *Toolkit for Water Policies and Governance: Converging Towards the OECD Council Recommendation on Water*, OECD Publishing, Paris, *https://doi.org/10.1787/ed1a7936-en*.

ISBN 978-92-64-65359-7 (print)
ISBN 978-92-64-87648-4 (pdf)

Photo credits: Cover © Olga Nikonova.

Corrigenda to publications may be found on line at: *www.oecd.org/about/publishing/corrigenda.htm*.

Preface

OECD's work on water started in the mid-1960s, focused on the science of environmental threats and technologies for assessing and monitoring them. Over the last 50 years, the OECD has continued to provide robust analyses and evidence-based policy recommendations to governments, elevating water as a driver for sustainable growth and expanding the scope and breadth of the work to cover water quantity and quality, access to water and sanitation services, water-related risks and disasters – including adaptation to a changing climate, as well as water governance and financing.

When I joined the OECD as Secretary-General in 2006, I endeavoured to further raise the profile of water at the OECD and in the global arena, as a strategic, cross-cutting concern. The intention was to transition from a sectoral to a multidisciplinary issue that drives sustainable and inclusive growth.

That resonated with the fact that in 2015, the global community adopted a Sustainable Development Goal on Clean Water and Sanitation (SDG 6), as part of the 2030 Agenda, thereby comforting OECD's foundational approach to water economics. The prevailing context today – marked by a pandemic with lasting consequences on the health of our communities and social and economic systems – is a stark reminder of the value of access to safe water for human livelihood.

In 2016, OECD member countries unanimously adopted a Council Recommendation on Water – a legal instrument to which practice accords great moral force as representing the political will of Adherents. The Recommendation is a concise and coherent international standard providing high-level policy guidance on the management of water resources and the delivery of water services.

In order to support the implementation of the Recommendation, this Toolkit collates good practices, policies and governance arrangements from countries that adhere to the Recommendation. I trust that it can inspire all levels of government in their efforts to realise their water-related goals and commitments, achieve SDG 6 and contribute to other global agendas such as the United Nations General Assembly Resolution on the human rights to safe drinking water and sanitation, the Paris Agreement, the Sendai Framework and the New Urban Agenda.

I also invite non-OECD countries to adhere to the OECD Council Recommendation on Water and enrich the experience captured in the toolkit. The OECD stands ready to accompany their transition towards water policies and governance that are fit for future challenges and that will contribute to better lives.

Angel Gurría
OECD Secretary-General

Foreword

The OECD has been providing governments with policy guidance on water over the last 50 years. That guidance builds on thorough analyses of water-related challenges, reviews of policy responses and governance arrangements, and intense consultation through OECD bodies and in other fora.

The Recommendation of the OECD Council on water is a legal instrument that captures and updates the main messages that derive from such a unique experience with water policies and governance. It was co-produced as part of the OECD Horizontal Water Programme, by the Directorates for Environment, Financial and Enterprise Affairs, Public Governance, Trade and Agriculture, and the Centre for Entrepreneurship, SMEs, Regions and Cities. This co-production reflects the cross-cutting nature of water issues and policies, the need to address trade-offs and to enhance coherence and co-ordination across policy areas and communities.

The Recommendation provides countries with a strategic approach to develop a coherent water management system that contributes to sustainable growth and development. It sets out high-level policy guidance for water resources management and the delivery of water services. It is structured in substantive sections on Water Policies, Managing Water Quantity, Improving Water Quality, Managing Water Risks and Disasters, Ensuring Good Water Governance, and Ensuring Sustainable Finance, Investment and Pricing for Water and Water Services.

The Recommendation is recognised as a source of inspiration for - national and subnational – governments, civil society and the private sector. Since its adoption, the OECD has collated good practices that can support its implementation. They are compiled in this Toolkit. The Toolkit is designed to inspire and support countries, which have either adhered to, are considering adhering to, or aim to converge towards the OECD standard.

The OECD Secretariat stands ready to work with countries, which aspire to adhere to the Recommendation. Adherence can build a momentum towards ambitious policy reforms. It can signal a political will to converge towards international good practices that support the achievement of ambitious water policy objectives.

Updates of the toolkit and guidance towards adherence to the Recommendation are available on the dedicated OECD webpage (www.oecd.org/water).

Acknowledgements

The Toolkit underwent an extensive and inclusive horizontal consultative process designed to ensure that each relevant OECD body contributes to its findings. It was developed with the active engagement and under the supervision of: the Environment Policy Committee (EPOC), the Committee for Agriculture (COAG), the Regional Development Policy Committee (RDPC) and its Water Governance Initiative (WGI), the Regulatory Policy Committee (RPC) and its Network of Economic Regulators (NER), the Public Governance Committee (PGC) and the Development Assistance Committee (DAC), as well as relevant stakeholders such as Business at OECD, Trade Union Advisory Committee (TUAC) and non-governmental environmental organisations (through the European Environmental Bureau). The delegates of these groups are gratefully acknowledged.

An Informal Water Liaison Group gathered permanent delegations to the OECD. It was brought together to discuss key milestones in the process and co-ordinate the Secretariat's interactions with experts from Adherent countries.

The process was steered by an inter-directorate working group, consisting of all members of the Secretariat of the OECD bodies, who co-produced the Toolkit. Catherine Gamper co-ordinated the whole process and Mikaela Rambali (both from the Environment Directorate) was the lead author and particularly instrumental in addressing comments received from delegates. The Toolkit was co-produced by a horizontal OECD team composed of Celine Kauffmann, Martha Baxter and Anna Pietikainen (economic regulation), Jack Radish and Charles Baubion (disasters and catastrophic risks) from the Public Governance Directorate; Guillaume Gruère and Makiko Shigemitsu (agriculture) from the Trade and Agriculture Directorate; Aziza Akhmouch and Oriana Romano (governance) from the Centre for Entrepreneurship, SMEs, Regions and Cities; Mamiko Yokoi-Arai and Leigh Wolfrom (financial affairs) from the Directorate for Financial and Enterprise Affairs. Section VI on Good Governance draws extensively on the 2018 report "Implementing the OECD Principles on Water Governance".

Xavier Leflaive supported the process, building on his experience with the negotiation of the Recommendation in 2016. Céline Folsché provided constructive legal advice. Brooke Demchuk helped with the dedicated survey. Ines Reale provided seamless administrative support. Anthony Cox, Deputy Director, Amy Plantin and Simon Buckle, Heads of Division, OECD Environment Directorate, ironed the final stages of the process.

The Secretariat gratefully acknowledges financial support from the Republic of Korea.

Table of contents

Preface 3

Foreword 4

Acknowledgements 5

Acronyms 10

Executive summary 11

1. Introduction 13
    References 16

2. General water policy 17
    2.1. Adjust water policies to local conditions 18
    2.2. Long-term water management planning 18
    2.3. Interlinkages between surface and groundwater management 21
    2.4. Reviews and updates 21
    2.5. Stakeholder consultation 22
    2.6. Joint management of water quantity and quality 22
    2.7. Address practices, trends and developments for water availability, demand and risks 24
    2.8. Facilitate the development and diffusion of innovation 25
    References 27
    Notes 28

3. Managing water quantity 29
    3.1. Water demand management policies 30
    3.2. Promoting water use efficiency 33
    3.3. Water allocation regimes 35
    3.4. Collective management approaches 39
    3.5. Improved knowledge and data 39
    References 41
    Notes 42

4. Improving water quality 43
    4.1. Allocation of resources to manage water pollution 44
    4.2. Risk mitigation 49
    4.3. Reduction of water pollution 49

4.4. Cost-effectiveness 50
4.5. Cost-effectiveness and Polluter Pays Principle 52
4.6. Compliance 53
4.7. Sustainable use of water-related ecosystems 55
4.8. Coherence between water and sectoral policies 55
References 58
Notes 60

5. Managing water risks and disasters 61
5.1. Managing water risks and disasters in a cooperative way 62
5.2. Risk assessment 63
5.3. Risk awareness 66
5.4. Setting and revising acceptable levels of water risk 68
5.5. Prevention and mitigation measures 69
5.6. Emergency response measures 72
5.7. Social policies and financial mechanisms 74
5.8. Transparency, accountability and public awareness 75
5.9. Policy coherence 75
5.10. Water risks related to climate change in agriculture 76
5.11. Water risks related to cities 77
References 79
Notes 80

6. Ensuring good water governance 81
6.1. Clearly allocate and distinguish roles and responsibilities 85
6.2. Manage water at the appropriate scale(s) 86
6.3. Encourage policy coherence and effective cross-sectoral co-ordination 87
6.4. Adapt the level of capacity to the complexity of water challenges 88
6.5. Use data and information to guide policy 89
6.6. Mobilise water finance efficiently 91
6.7. Implement and enforce water regulation 91
6.8. Promote innovative water governance practices 93
6.9. Mainstream integrity and transparency 95
6.10. Promote stakeholder engagement 95
6.11. Manage governance complexity and trade-offs 99
6.12. Monitor and evaluate water policy and governance 99
References 101
Notes 102

7. Ensuring sustainable finance, investment and pricing for water and water services 103
7.1. Principles for financing water resources management 105
7.2. Aiming for the greatest social returns to investment 108
7.3. Diversifying revenue streams and tapping into new sources of capital 111
References 116
Notes 117

8. Pricing instruments for water management and services 118
8.1. Setting abstraction charges that reflect water scarcity 119
8.2. Setting water pollution charges to incentivise pollution prevention 122
8.3. Setting tariffs that cover operation, maintenance and renewal costs 123

8.4. Accounting for the redistributive consequences and priority water uses 124
8.5. Phasing out price-distorting policy measures and general subsidies 127
8.6. Transaction costs 129
References 130
Notes 131

Tables

Table 2.1. Top Water-Related Inventor Countries, 1990-2015 25
Table 6.1. Governance Arrangements in Water Regulators 93
Table 8.1. The use of abstraction charges for ground and surface water 120
Table 8.2. Examples of features of pollution charges in selected Adherents 123
Table 8.3. Water cost recovery in agriculture 124
Table 8.4. Examples of subsidies in water services and water resources management 127

Figures

Figure 2.1. Uncertainties about future water availability and demand in national management plans 19
Figure 2.2. Types of uncertainties considered in water management planning 20
Figure 2.3. Reporting on implementation of national water management plans 21
Figure 2.4. Issues covered in national water management plans 23
Figure 3.1. Global water demand, 2000-2050 30
Figure 3.2. Environmental flows and sustainable diversion limits in water allocation mechanisms 32
Figure 3.3. Key considerations for defining environmental flows 33
Figure 3.4. Sequence of priority uses in water allocation among selected Adherents 37
Figure 3.5. Data sources to facilitate water quantity management 40
Figure 4.1. Key pollutants of concern coming from the agricultural sector 46
Figure 4.2. Countries with effluent discharge tax 53
Figure 4.3. Types of penalties used in case of non-compliance with water quality regulation 55
Figure 4.4. Alignment of agriculture and water policies with section 4 recommendations on water quality 56
Figure 5.1. Number of water-related and non-water-related disasters in OECD countries 62
Figure 5.2. Actions taken to assess water-related risks 64
Figure 5.3. Coverage of risk assessments at the basin/local level 65
Figure 5.4. Actions to raise awareness of exposure to water-related risks 67
Figure 5.5. Actors with formal responsibilities for risk communication 68
Figure 5.6. Actions to reduce water-related risks through prevention and mitigation measures 70
Figure 5.7. Level of awareness, technical capacity and implementation progress for NbS 71
Figure 5.8. Emergency preparedness and response measures for water related risks 73
Figure 5.9. Focus of major public funded research related to water availability to agriculture 76
Figure 6.1. Overview of OECD Principles on Water Governance 82
Figure 6.2. The OECD Water Governance Indicator Framework 83
Figure 6.3. A ten-step assessment framework 84
Figure 6.4. Map of the pilots and evolving practices 84
Figure 6.5. Coherence between water management and other sectoral plans 88
Figure 6.6. Status of water regulatory agencies in selected OECD and non-OECD Adherents 92
Figure 6.7. Levels of stakeholder engagement 97
Figure 7.1. Funding strategies for water management plans 104
Figure 7.2. Distance to compliance with the EU Directives on Drinking Water and Urban Wastewater Treatment 105
Figure 7.3. Consideration of principles for financing water resources management 106
Figure 7.4. Domains using ecosystem-based approaches 109
Figure 7.5. Adherents' sources of financing for water management 112
Figure 7.6. Public budgets and household water tariffs as sources of funding for water management 113
Figure 7.7. Share of EU funding in estimated total expenditures for water supply and sanitation 114
Figure 8.1. Average alignment of agriculture and water policies with section 8 of the Recommendation on Water 119
Figure 8.2. Reflecting water scarcity in water charges 121

Figure 8.3. Mechanisms to address affordability issues for water and sanitation services for low-income households 125
Figure 8.4. Mechanisms to address affordability issues 125
Figure 8.5. Share of water supply and sanitation expenditures in households' disposable income 126
Figure 8.6. Agriculture support in percentage of gross farm receipts 128
Figure 8.7. Irrigation related producer support estimates (1986-2016) 129

Boxes

Box 1.1. Purpose and scope of the OECD Recommendation on Water 15
Box 2.1. A national reform to address institutional and financial inefficiency of national water management in Korea 24
Box 2.2. The use of citizen science and public engagement to enhance water-related information 26
Box 3.1. Water allocation systems at a River Basin District level in Spain 36
Box 4.1. Identifying and prioritising indicator substances for contaminant of emerging concerns monitoring in Switzerland 45
Box 4.2. Nutrient modelling in New Zealand 47
Box 4.3. The collaborative governance model of the Canterbury Water Management Strategy (CWMS), New Zealand 48
Box 4.4. Joint management of water quality in North America's Great Lakes 50
Box 4.5. Identified measures to reduce pharmaceutical residues at different stages of the pharmaceutical chain in the Netherlands 51
Box 5.1. The use of ecosystem-based approaches to manage water-related risks 71
Box 6.1. OECD Principles on Water Governance 82
Box 6.2. Stakeholder engagement 96
Box 7.1. Strengthening the application of the polluter pays principle in the European Union 107
Box 7.2. Recovering costs of advanced wastewater treatment plant upgrades, Germany 107
Box 8.1. Denmark's experience in considering price elasticity of water demand 127

Acronyms

CEC	Contaminant of emerging concerns
AI	Artificial intelligence
BOD	Biochemical oxygen demand
COAG	Committee for Agriculture
DAC	Development Assistance Committee
EIA	Environmental Impact Assessment
EPOC	Environment Policy Committee
EPR	Extended Producer Responsibility
E-PRTR	European Pollutant Release and Transfer Register
ERSAR	Water and Waste Services Regulation Authority (Portugal)
EU	European Union
GIS	Geographic Information System
HLRF	High-Level Risk Forum
IBT	Increasing block tariffs
ICT	Information and communication technology
JWPAE	Joint Working Party on Agriculture and Environment
NbS	Nature-based solutions
O&M	Operation and maintenance
OFWAT	Water Services Regulation Authority (United Kingdom)
PGC	Public Governance Committee
RBMP	River basin management plan
RDPC	Regional Development Policy Committee
RPC	Regulatory Policy Committee
RTA	Relative technological advantage
SDG	Sustainable Development Goals
SEA	Strategic Environmental Assessment
TMDL	Total Maximum Daily Load
TUAC	Trade Union Advisory Committee
UK	United Kingdom
US	United States
UWWTD	Urban Waste Water Treatment Directive
WFD	Water Framework Directive
WGI	Water Governance Initiative

Executive summary

In 2020, the COVID-19 crisis was a stark reminder of how critical access to safe water is for human health and livelihood and consequently for sustainable and inclusive development. With 2.1 billion people without access to safe water services and over 4.4 billion lacking access to safe sanitation, the world is not on track to meet its global commitments on water, most notably the Sustainable Development Goal on clean water and sanitation and the United Nations General Assembly Resolution on the human rights to safe drinking water and sanitation. Climate change only adds to the challenge. Due to the cross-sectoral and strategic nature of water, failure to deliver on water commitments is consequential for the achievement of other global agendas such as the 2030 Agenda, the Paris Agreement, the Sendai Framework and the New Urban Agenda.

The OECD Council Recommendation on water is a concise and coherent international standard that provides high-level policy guidance on the management of water resources and the delivery of water services. In addition to cross-cutting general principles, it focuses on managing water quantity, improving water quality, managing water risks and disasters, ensuring good water governance and ensuring finance, investment and pricing for water and water services.

Since its adoption by all OECD members in December 2016, the Recommendation has been recognised and valued as a source of inspiration for countries that adhered to it. It has helped several Adherents and non-Adherents think about water management more strategically and holistically to make policies and funding strategies more coherent across different policy areas. The Recommendation also served as a reference for other communities such as civil society and the private sector.

The Recommendation provides the analytical framework for demand-driven, country-specific policy dialogues, which aim to strengthen the policy and institutional frameworks for water management. For instance, it provided the backbone for the most recent water policy dialogues in Argentina, Brazil, Georgia, Kazakhstan, Korea, Moldova, and Peru. In each of these countries, sections of the Recommendation were used to assess the performance of water policies against best practices and provide tailored guidance to improve them with a view to align with the ambition and the substance of the Recommendation.

This Toolkit aims to support the implementation of the Recommendation. It documents a wide range of initiatives and practices in place in adhering countries, which are well-aligned with the ambition and the substance of the Recommendation, offering practical examples on how the Recommendation can be applied.

The Toolkit highlights area where Adherents have made significant progress towards the ambition of the Recommendation. In particular, Adherents generally have set long-term water planning instruments that consider the different and often uncertain factors that influence future water demand, water availability and exposure to water-related risks. All Adherents have adopted water efficiency measures, and there have been significant reforms of water allocation regimes to make them fit for future challenges. Similarly, all Adherents have made significant investments in maintaining or improving water quality levels, considering different water uses and emerging concerns. A broad adoption of good practices to identify, assess and reduce exposure to water related risks can be observed, with several Adherents promoting a holistic approach to sharing and managing these risks. Moreover, most Adherents have applied the *OECD Principles on Water Governance* (which were embodied verbatim in Section VI of the Recommendation) to improve institutional and regulatory frameworks across different scales, stakeholders and sectors. Finally, the Toolkit documents practices in the design of economic policy instruments to manage water use efficiently and in an equitable manner, and the adoption of other financing mechanisms to meet investment needs.

The Toolkit also documents significant challenges that Adherents face in making further progress in implementing the Recommendation. For example, in effectively and continuously engaging stakeholders in water management planning processes. Moreover, although the usefulness and effectiveness of jointly managing water quality and quantity is recognised, actual good practices (such as nature-based solutions) are lagging behind. Similarly, water efficiency is affected by distorting incentives to use more water, even in stressed areas (e.g. for agriculture). Monitoring capacities for many contaminants are still lacking and investment in improving water quality is constrained. Additionally, coastal risks are not as well assessed and monitored as other water-related risks, even though their damage potential could be significantly higher. Finally, there is room to further improve the design and use of economic policy instruments, in alignment with the Polluter Pays principle and the Beneficiary Pays principle, and to disseminate promising financing mechanisms to meet investments needs (including proven models and innovative approaches, such as blended finance).

To support identified areas of improvement, the Toolkit suggests that three sets of issues could be explored to further facilitate Adherents' alignment with the ambition of the Recommendation. The first relates to the management of intensifying water challenges due to a changing climate, the risk of the conjunction of multiple crises (such as flood risks and a pandemic) and the interface between water and health. The second set of issues relates to the increase in projected investment needs to cope with these emerging challenges at a time of increased pressure on public finance. The third relates to the important role of data and information, where Adherents would benefit from concrete guidance on how new sources of data, analytics and artificial intelligence may be better able to support water agendas, policies and governance. These issues provide food for thought for further collaboration towards the development of good practices in line with the ambition of the Recommendation.

The Toolkit is meant to be a living document. It will be enriched by new developments in Adherent countries and will also benefit from the experience of countries, which will adhere to the Recommendation. As such, the Toolkit provides opportunities for further exchange, capacity building, and thereby can accelerate the adoption of policies, governance and practices that contribute to water security and sustainable growth.

1. Introduction

This opening chapter introduces the OECD Council Recommendation on Water, its purpose and scope. It presents the objective of the Toolkit and outlines its main sections.

The Toolkit for Water Policies and Governance (hereafter the "Toolkit") compiles policies, governance arrangements and related tools that facilitate the design and implementation of water management practices in line with the OECD Council Recommendation on Water (OECD, 2016[1]). It is designed to inspire and support countries, which have either adhered to, are considering adhering to, or aim to converge towards the OECD standard.

The Recommendation of the OECD Council on Water [OECD/LEGAL/0434] (hereafter the "Recommendation") was adopted by the OECD Council in December 2016. The adoption marked the outcome of a 2-year consultation process. It involved delegates from ministries active in the fields of agriculture, development assistance, environment, public governance, regional development, and regulatory policy, as well as with relevant stakeholders (the business sector, trade unions, environmental organisations) and the OECD Water Governance Initiative.

The Recommendation puts forward a concise and coherent international standard providing high-level policy guidance on a range of topics relevant for water resources management and the delivery of water services: managing water quantity, improving water quality, managing water risks and disasters, ensuring good water governance as well as sustainable finance, investment and pricing for water services. Box 1.1 provides a description of the purpose and scope of the Recommendation. The Recommendation is available in English and French (OECD official languages) and in Portuguese and Spanish.

To date, all OECD members are Adherents to the Recommendation. Cabo Verde is the first non-OECD member country to adhere to the Recommendation. The adherence of other countries is pending.

The Toolkit provides tools and good practices in place, for each section of the Recommendation. It was developed as part of a reporting process for the OECD Council, referred to as "the Council" in subsequent chapters. Since the adoption of the Recommendation, the OECD has provided a platform to exchange policies, practices and lessons learned. The tools and good practices compiled derive from these exchanges. The Toolkit documents a wide range of initiatives and practices, which are well-aligned with the ambition and the substance of the Recommendation.

The outline of the Toolkit follows the substantive sections of the Recommendation, covering water policies (Section 2), managing water quantity (Section 3), improving water quality (Section 4), managing water risks and disasters (Section 5), ensuring good water governance (Section 6), as well as ensuring sustainable finance, investment and pricing for water and water services (Sections 7 and 8).

Box 1.1. Purpose and scope of the OECD Recommendation on Water

The effective and efficient management of water resources and water services remains a major challenge for countries around the world, and pressures on water resources continue to mount. The inclusion of water as one of the Sustainable Development Goals (SDG 6) and its prominence in a range of other SDGs reflect the importance that the global community places on water.

The objective of the Recommendation is to provide Adherents with a strategic approach to develop a coherent water management system that contributes to sustainable growth and development. It sets out high-level policy guidance for water resources management and the delivery of water services.

The Recommendation captures and updates the main messages that derived from earlier recommendations and OECD work on water, including the 2015 OECD Principles on Water Governance, which are reflected in its section 6.

The Recommendation is structured in seven substantive sections:

- Water Policies (Section 2)
- Managing Water Quantity (Section 3)
- Improving Water Quality (Section 4)
- Managing Water Risks And Disasters (Section 5)
- Ensuring Good Water Governance (Section 6)
- Ensuring Sustainable Finance, Investment and Pricing for Water and Water Services (Sections 7 and 8).

Source: https://legalinstruments.oecd.org/en/instruments/OECD-LEGAL-0434

References

OECD (2019), *Pharmaceutical Residues in Freshwater: Hazards and Policy Responses*, OECD Studies on Water, OECD Publishing, Paris, https://dx.doi.org/10.1787/c936f42d-en. [3]

OECD (2016), *OECD Legal Instrument: Recommendation of the Council on Water*, https://legalinstruments.oecd.org/en/instruments/OECD-LEGAL-0434. [1]

OECD, FAO, IIASA (2020), *Towards a G20 Action Plan on Water. Background note to the G20 Saudi Presidency*. [2]

2. General water policy

This chapter explores how Adherents adjust water policies to local conditions. It provides examples of long-term water management planning, including plans' review and updates as well as stakeholder consultation. It also illustrates how Adherents manage the interlinkages between surface and groundwater. It describes efforts to manage water quantity and quality jointly as well as to address practices, trends and developments that affect water availability, demand and risks. Finally, the chapter covers the development and diffusion of innovation.

The first section of the Recommendation sets out a set of generic and cross-cutting recommendations for Adherents to set up and implement water policies:

2.1. Adjust water policies to local conditions

The first part of the Recommendation asks Adherents to set up and implement water policies that "are adjusted to local conditions". This requires acknowledging the peculiarities of geographical, cultural, political systems at appropriate scales. This can be done in two ways, which are outlined below. The issue is revisited in chapter 6, on water governance.

The first way is to adjust water management to local conditions. In that context, vertical co-ordination between the different scales is key. As regards scale, many countries ensure institutions are set up in line with that focus. For example, **France** established six water basin agencies in 1964 on its mainland, to increase the understanding of local concerns for water management and to ensure administrative boundaries follow a hydrographical logic. In the **European Union**, the Water Framework Directive encouraged the integration and centralisation of all water management activities at the river basin level (European Union, 2000[1]). Other countries consider catchments as the appropriate geographical scale for water management (Austria, Germany). This decentralisation concept was implemented via the requirement to develop cross regional and cross border river basin management plans. Chapter 6 (on governance) provides illustrations on how to achieve vertical co-ordination.

The second way is to adjust policy instruments (e.g. abstraction charges) to local conditions. For instance, abstraction charges are often differentiated by hydrographic zones, so as to send an adequate signal on the value of water and to consider equity. In **Canada,** for instance, the abstraction charges are defined at the provincial level (see further details in chapter 8). Similarly, charges may also have to be differentiated geographically to adequately address different environmental externalities (OECD, 2017[2]). In **Portugal**, the Water Resources Tax in place since 2008 is differentiated by sector and region and is updated regularly. In **Europe**, the Urban Wastewater Treatment Directive set distinctively stringent standards for wastewater treatment in sensitive areas, e.g. where the dilution capacity is low or where water is used for recreational purposes (European Union, 1991[3]).

Local conditions fluctuate over time. In **Australia,** tradable entitlements define access rights to an ongoing share of water within a consumptive pool and water allocation changes according to seasonal water availability in the consumptive pool (allocations) (OECD, 2019[4]) (see chapter 4 for further details).

2.2. Long-term water management planning

The second part of the Recommendation on water policies asks Adherents to set up and implement water policies that "are based on long term water management plans, preferably at river basin, or aquifer level, and, as appropriate, in a transboundary framework. Such plans should foster conjunctive management of surface and groundwater, and be regularly reviewed and updated". The 2019 OECD Implementation Survey shows that almost all 27 respondents have a national water management plan in place. Federal countries are a case in point, as plans may be defined at sub-national level, when water management is not a federal issue.

The **EU** Water Framework Directive, which calls for the long-term protection of available water resources, requires its member states to carry out assessment of long-term changes in natural conditions (European Union, 2000[1]). As reported by the European Commission, the first official draft River Basin Management Plan (RBMP) had to be presented by the end of 2008. To date, all member states have approved their RBMPs and almost all EU member states reported their second RBMPs for the period 2015-2021 to the European Commission under the Water Framework Directive. The information in the RBMPs is available on the common digital repository WISE[1]: the maps include the River Basin Districts and their sub-units, the surface water bodies (water body category, ecological status or potential and chemical status), the groundwater bodies (aquifer type, quantitative status and chemical status) and the monitoring sites.

A key characteristic of long-term planning is uncertainty. The 2019 OECD Implementation Survey shows that 22 out of 26 responding Adherents consider uncertainties in planning for future water availability and demand (Figure 2.1).

Figure 2.1. Uncertainties about future water availability and demand in national management plans

Note: Responses to the question "Does the national water management plan consider uncertainties about future water availability and demand?".
Source: 2019 survey on the implementation of the OECD Council Recommendation on Water; 27 responses received, including 26 Adherents.

Of those Adherents that consider uncertainty in their planning, nearly 70% take into account climate as well as water demand scenarios and equally 70% consider water-related risks (Figure 2.2). However, the OECD Survey on water and agriculture policy changes carried out in 2019 showed that of those Adherents that set quantified national planning targets for the use of water resources in the agriculture sector, only 41% account for climate change. More work is needed to assess how countries design and reflect scenarios on climate change and future water availability in planning instruments. Indeed, future local and regional changes in precipitation are uncertain, as different climate models project different directions of change for some regions.

Figure 2.2. Types of uncertainties considered in water management planning

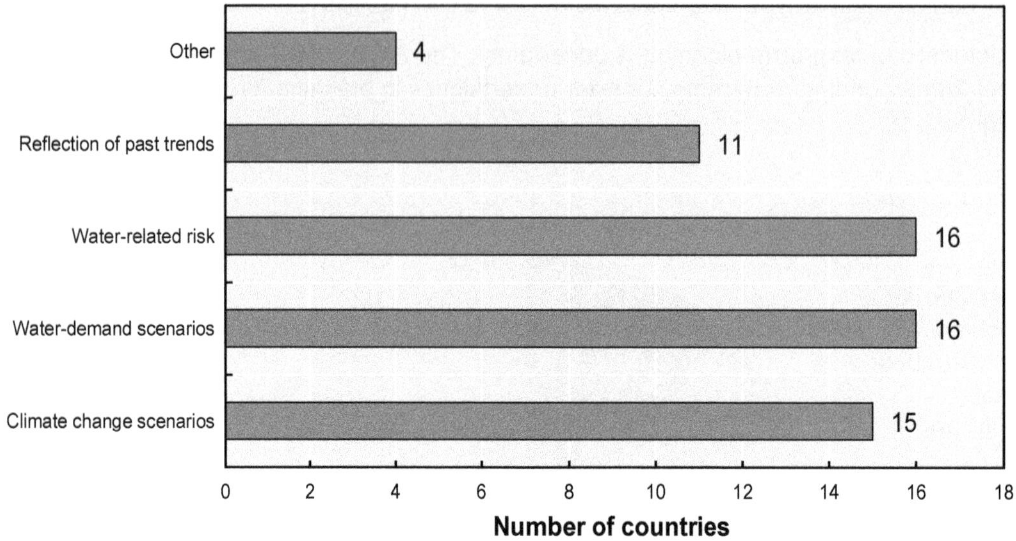

Note: Responses to the question: "How does the national water management plan reflect uncertainties about future water availability and demand?". Multiple responses were possible.
Source: 2019 survey on the implementation of the OECD Council Recommendation on Water; 27 responses received, including 26 Adherents.

Turkey has made efforts to improve its modelling of future climate using scenarios based on expected medium to high global temperatures (RCP4.5 and RCP8.5). It uses three global climate models downscaled to 20 km, which help to identify local changes. Turkey also considers the impact of increasing temperatures and variabilities in precipitation levels, and does so for a horizon until the end of the 21st century (OECD, 2019[5]). River basin agencies in France drafted strategic plans to adapt to climate change, a priority of the on-going programming period. In Chile, some river management plans consider the impacts of climate change, such as those for the rivers Maule and Maipo. Efforts are underway to integrate surface and groundwater modelling in forthcoming river management plans (OECD, 2019[6]). Spain is addressing uncertainties in long-term water conditions by improving its climate models and updating its mapping of water bodies accordingly. Models incorporate a long time series of historical data and make ambitious projections of future water availability[2] (OECD, 2019[6]).

The Delta Programme of the **Netherlands** aims to ensure that present and future generations are safe from water and will have sufficient freshwater in the centuries ahead. The programme takes an "adaptive delta management" approach, taking measures in the short term that will expand capacity to adapt to long-term changes and withstand extreme situations. The programme is supported by a dedicated Delta fund, which secures financial resources for implementation (OECD, 2013[7]).

More work is required to assess whether river basin management plans factor in shifting conditions that affect water availability and use and exposure to water-related risks (see also chapter 3); if plans are aligned with projected plans in other domains (e.g. land use and urban development, agriculture development, energy supply); if they are supported by robust financing strategies; and if they drive decisions related to water management and investment.

2.3. Interlinkages between surface and groundwater management

Alongside long term planning, the Recommendation calls for Adherents to foster "conjunctive management of surface and groundwater".

This is an approach followed by **Australia** in its National Water Initiative, which was adopted in the midst a prolonged drought (1996-2010). The National Water Initiative acknowledges the connectivity between surface and groundwater and calls for conjunct management of these systems (OECD, 2018[8]). It also reminds that jurisdictions need to ensure that local environmental flow management and environmental objectives (e.g. on water quality, habitat and pest management) are coherent across complementary waterways (OECD, 2019[4]). Successful implementation of this principle can be seen at the local level. For instance, in the State of California (**United States**), the Arvin Edison Water and Storage District has engaged in conjunctive management, storing groundwater during wet years and pumping back during dry seasons, creating measurable benefits for users (OECD, 2015[9]).

2.4. Reviews and updates

The Council also recommends that Adherents' long-term water management plans are "regularly reviewed and updated". This notion is also reflected in the OECD Water Governance Principles (chapter 6), which call for regular monitoring and evaluation of water policies. The following section presents examples for the national level, which are also relevant for all levels of governance.

The great majority of respondents, namely 92% of those that responded 'yes' to having a national water management plan in the 2019 OECD Implementation Survey, have an obligation to report on the implementation of the plan or equivalent (for countries with plans at sub-national level). Of those respondents that have such an obligation, 72% have quantitative targets to track implementation (Figure 2.3). **EU** member states have formal requirements to undertake monitoring and evaluation of the implementation of their River Basin Management Plans, which are updated every six years. In addition to doing so for its 25 River Basin Management Plans, **Spain** publishes an annual report as part of this reporting exercise. Some countries, including **France**, report on qualitative objectives as well.

Figure 2.3. Reporting on implementation of national water management plans

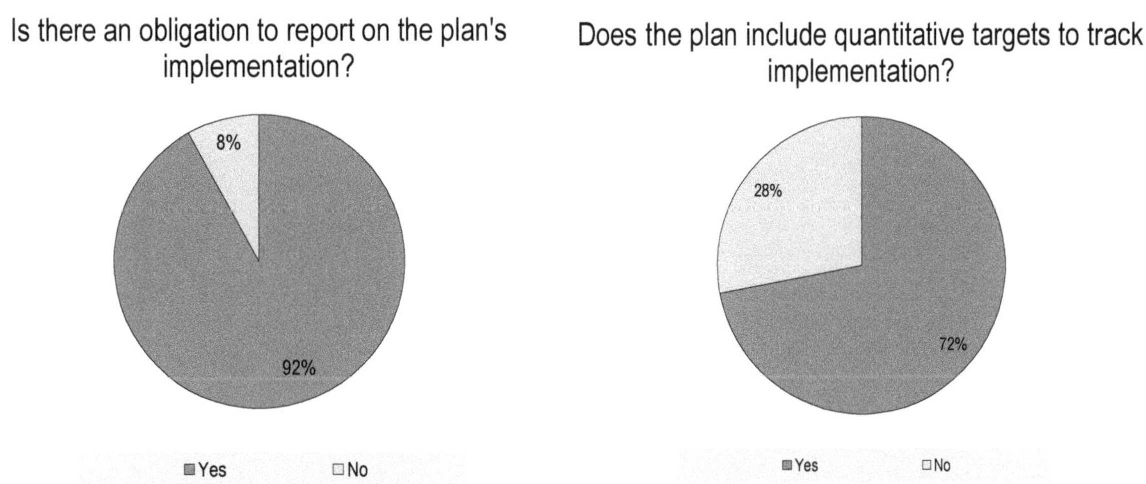

Note: Responses to the questions: "Is there an obligation to report on the plan's implementation?" and "Does the plan include quantitative targets to track implementation?"

Source: 2019 survey on the implementation of the OECD Council Recommendation on Water; 25 responses received, including 24 Adherents.

2.5. Stakeholder consultation

Finally, with regard to long term water management planning and conjunctive water management, the Recommendation claims that water policies "would benefit from stakeholder consultation". This echoes the principle 10 in section 6 of the Recommendation, which promotes stakeholder engagement in water management at large.

There are an increasing number of examples of legislation, guidelines and standards that formalise stakeholder engagement to encourage information sharing, co-operation, consultation or awareness raising into operational rules and procedures. Indeed, according to Article 14 of the **EU** Water Framework Directive, consultations with the public should be carried out throughout the different steps of development of the river basin management plans. The state of Baden-Württemberg (**Germany**) involved key stakeholders through a series of over 70 different local events to produce a water management plan.

However, barriers remain in practice such as "consultation fatigue", often due to a lack of clarity on how to use stakeholder inputs in decision making and implementation. Among other shortcomings that have been identified are insufficient time, staff and funding, weak supportive legal frameworks, consultation "capture" from over-represented categories, weak capacity, the lack of public concern and awareness, information asymmetry, fragmented institutional settings, and the complexity of the issues (OECD, 2015[10]).

2.6. Joint management of water quantity and quality

The Council recommends that Adherents set up and implement water policies that "encourage the joint management of water quantity and quality, and pay attention to the hydro morphological characteristics and temporal variability of water bodies, as these affect water quantity, quality, disasters, and water-related ecosystems".

The 2019 OECD Implementation Survey shows that countries have adopted national water management plans covering a range of issues, to ensure coordination across water-related policies (Figure 2.4). These areas usually cover water quantity and quality, exposure to water-related risks, access to water and sanitation services as well as investment in infrastructure.

Figure 2.4. Issues covered in national water management plans

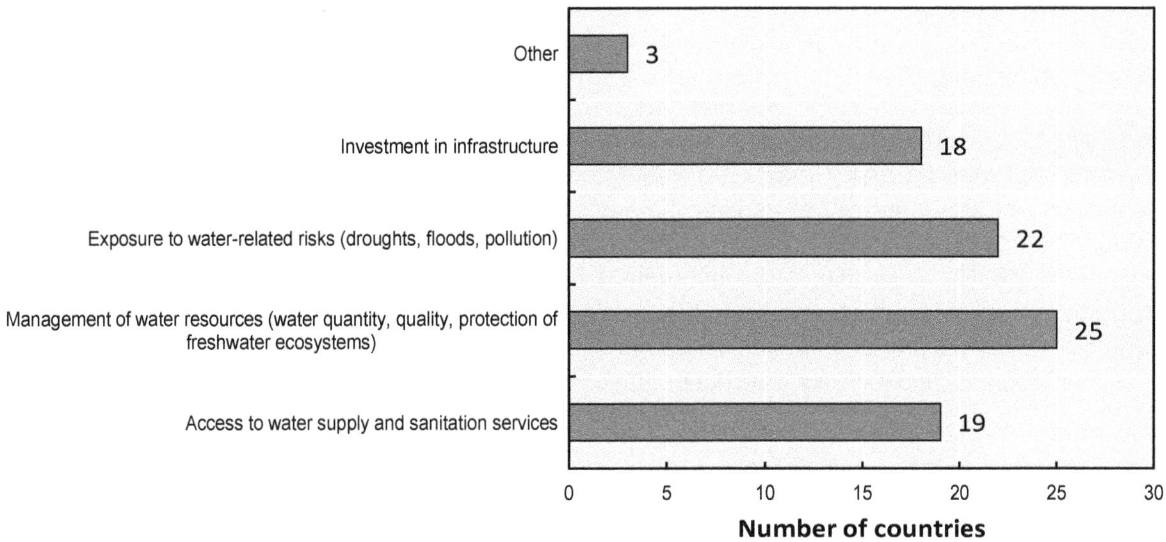

Note: Responses to the question: "Which of the following topics are covered in your country's national water management plan?", "Other" includes: irrigation, water finance, R&D, water industry, international cooperation; drinking water; analysis of pressures and impact on water resources by different users. Multiple responses were possible.
Source: 2019 survey on the implementation of the OECD Council Recommendation on Water; 25 responses received, including 24 Adherents.

In the **EU** Water Framework Directive, joint management of water quantity and quality is promoted through the RBMPs. The plans are a detailed account of how the objectives set for the river basin (ecological status, quantitative status, chemical status and protected area objectives) are going to be met. Ecological status is based on biological quality elements and supporting physico-chemical and hydro morphological quality elements (European Union, 2000[1]). In **Israel**, water quality and quantity are intrinsically related in the management of water resources, as the country uses desalinated seawater as a key source of water supply and treated wastewater as a major source of water for irrigation, to reduce the need for and use of freshwater extraction from aquifers and surface water bodies. Co-ordination is ensured under the Water Authority Council, set up in 2007, and responsible for all decision making and policy setting by the Israeli Water authority.

The use of nature-based solutions (NbS) is a promising approach to deliver on both water quantity and quality objectives. For example, the "Upstream Thinking" catchment management scheme in the **United Kingdom** has successfully restored over 2000 hectares of sensitive upstream land on Exmoor in 2010-15 to improve peatland and biodiversity, and reduce sediment loads and flood risk downstream. The work is targeted to benefit 15 water treatment facilities supplying 72% of the total daily water to customers in the region (OECD, 2017[11]). The use of NbS have been promoted in Europe, with EU Horizon 2020 framework programme for research and innovation allocating approximately EUR 185 million to research and pilot projects between 2014 and 2020 (European Parliament, 2017[12]).

Inter-institutional committees can facilitate the management of various water-related issues and ensure policy coherence across national authorities responsible for water and other policies. In **Ireland**, the Water Policy Advisory Committee co-ordinates the overlap between the EU Water Framework Directive, and other directives including the Floods Directive and Marine Framework Directive. In **Costa Rica**, there are committees on hydrology and meteorology, groundwater, surface water and wastewater. Some countries have merged the responsibilities for water and environment such as some states in **Brazil**. In **Korea**, the Government Organisation Act, June 2018, merges the vast majority of responsibilities for water quantity and quality management under the Ministry of Environment (OECD, 2018[13]) (Box 2.1). See chapter 6 for further arrangements that support policy coherence in water management.

Box 2.1. A national reform to address institutional and financial inefficiency of national water management in Korea

Korea's efforts to address institutional and financial inefficiency of national water management policies have translated into the policy reform for integrated water management. In 2018, the Government Organisation Act was amended to transfer the authority over water resources conservation, use, and development from the Ministry of Land, Infrastructure, and Transport (MOLIT) to the Ministry of Environment (MOE). With this, 188 government officials from the MOLIT with a water quantity management budget of over 500 million USD and 5 878 staff members from K-water (asset value of about 9 billion USD) to the MOE. In addition, authorities overseeing groundwater quantity and quality as well as multi-regional and local waterworks management, were integrated into the MOE.

Moreover, the Framework Act on Water Management was introduced for the first time in the history of the Korean government in 2018, laying legal foundation for the integrated water management encompassing water quality and quantity management. The Framework Act on Water Management, remaining in force since June 2019, covers 12 basic principles on water management including publicness of water, sound water cycle, management by basin, integrated water management, management of water demand, addressing climate change, and multi-stakeholder participation, along with the National Master Plan for Water Management and the Comprehensive Basin Water Management Plans.

Following the introduction of the Framework Act on Water Management, the Presidential Water Commission and four Basin Water Commissions were established. Overseen by the Office of the President, the Presidential Water Commission is chaired by the Prime Minister, and a civic expert appointed by the President. A majority of the total number of members of the Commission must be comprised of civic members other than ex-officio members with appropriate gender ratio.

The National Master Plan for Water Management for the next decade, the first ever inter-governmental plan for water management strategies, and the Comprehensive Basin Water Management Plans are expected to be completed by June 2021 and June 2022 respectively. These plans must be adjusted based on the results of validity assessment which will be conducted on a 5-year basis and are subject to annual implementation reviews. The Presidential and Basin Water Commissions will discuss, review and co-ordinate several laws and plans set by Korean ministries and local governments in order to ensure policy coherence and efficiency.

Source: (Republic of Korea, 2019[14]) (Republic of Korea, 2020[15])

2.7. Address practices, trends and developments for water availability, demand and risks

Further to the joint management of water quantity and quality, the Council recommends Adherents to "address practices, trends and developments that affect water availability, water demand, and exposure and vulnerability to water risks; reflect their wider economics, social and environmental consequences, at different scales". See further details on the management of water quantity in chapter 3, and on water risks in chapter 5, and on pricing instruments in chapter 8.

2.8. Facilitate the development and diffusion of innovation

The Council recommends that Adherents set up and implement water policies that "facilitate the development and diffusion of innovative and more efficient ways to manage water, based on technical and non-technical innovations".

Technical innovations exist in different domains related to water, notably pollution abatement (e.g. wastewater treatment), demand-side management (e.g. indoor or irrigation water conservation such as drip irrigation or leak prevention technologies) and supply-side management (e.g. rain water collection, desalination of sea and brackish water) (Haščič and Migotto, 2015[16]). There are also technical innovations in information and communications technology (ICT) such as smart meters that are beneficial to the water sector (Box 2.2).

Patent data for water-related technologies, used to explore the development of inventions, show that several Adherent countries are leading water innovation, namely the **United States**, accounting for more than 30% of global water-related technologies patenting in the period 1990-2015, followed by **Korea**, **Germany** and **Japan** (Table 2.1). **Korea** experienced rapid growth in the share of patenting, for water-related and all technologies, from less than 1% of the world's water-related patents in 1990 to more than a quarter since 2009. It is also notable that **Israel** has the highest share of demand-side water patents and a relatively larger share of high-value inventions that are transferable to other countries (Leflaive, Krieble and Smythe, 2020[17]).

Table 2.1. Top Water-Related Inventor Countries, 1990-2015

Country	United States	Korea	Germany	Japan	United Kingdom	France	Canada	Switzerland
Share of global water-related technologies (total patents)	30.90%	14.50%	12.00%	6.90%	4.60%	4.00%	2.50%	1.90%
Relative Technological Advantage (RTA)	1.14	0.97	1.22	0.48	1.85	1.55	1.45	2.05

Note: Water-related patented inventions include water pollution abatement or demand- or supply-side technologies.
Source: (Leflaive, Krieble and Smythe, 2020[17]).

When considering relative technological advantage (RTA), which measures a country's specialisation in a particular technological domain, **Switzerland** has a RTA of 2.05, indicating it is relatively specialised in water security technologies compared to other domains. Conversely, **Japan** with a RTA of 0.48 is 'underweight' in water related patenting relative to other areas of invention. Some Adherent countries, such as **Chile**, **or Australia**, are highly specialised in water-related technologies, which represent a high share of their domestic patenting. They are both top inventors and potential markets for the technology patented (Leflaive, Krieble and Smythe, 2020[17]). Different dynamics across countries, and relative specialisation of selected countries indicate that Adherents differ in the strategies developed and implemented to support and accelerate the development of water-related innovation.

Countries have also used different mechanisms to facilitate the diffusion of water related innovation. This encompassed the formation of groups in charge of transferring and knowledge and publicly available data. For instance, **New Zealand** established a Science and Technical Advisory Group to oversee the scientific evidence for freshwater policy development, and developed the Land Air Water Aotearoa (LAWA) – publicly sharing environmental data and information to help communities balance using natural resources while maintaining water quality and availability. The **EU** Commission set up a knowledge hub on agriculture and water management, aiming at providing links to available information from research in this area.[3]

The development and deployment of smart water systems has been encouraged by a number of Adherents such as **Australia, France, Israel, Korea** and the **Netherlands** as well as states (Arizona, California in the **United States** and Ontario in **Canada**). They have been deployed in combination with water tariff reforms and implementation of measures to encourage efficiency. In Arizona, water utilities adopted smart water meters to inform customers about their water usage. New smart water companies have emerged in **Ontario** and **Israel**. In **France**, incentives to reduce leakage in water supply and sanitation networks have driven the diffusion of smart meters and investment in data monitoring to detect and locate anomalies in real time (OECD, 2017[2]).

Non-technical innovations can help change behaviours to use water more efficiently (see section Promoting water use efficiency).

Box 2.2. The use of citizen science and public engagement to enhance water-related information

Citizen science, which is the involvement of citizens in scientific research and/or knowledge production, is an emerging example of a non-conventional data source that can play an important role in the process of monitoring water resources. The development of new technologies, such as smartphone apps and social networks, has broadened the scope of citizen contributions, enabling scientists to process far higher volumes of data than would previously have been possible. There are now many examples of citizen science projects around the world covering a diversity of domains including the water sector. For example, SciStarter.org is a search engine for citizen-science projects; and an inventory of citizen-science activities in Europe that address environmental policies was recently published.

Several mobile applications have been developed to facilitate the engagement of citizens in documenting and sharing information for the purpose of water resources monitoring. Examples include Citclops's EyeOnWater and Earthwatch's FreshWater Watch, which enable volunteers to contribute data on the colour of coastal waters, serving as a simple and accessible indicator for eutrophication that can be used together with remote-sensing data. NASA is exploring a potential of citizen science within general aviation to contribute aerial photos to assess eutrophication. A comparison of citizen science data and agency monitoring of water quality in the UK shows that FreshWater Watch data complements environmental agency monitoring efforts by filling in gaps in the spatial and temporal coverage, as well as water body types.

While not all citizen science programmes are designed or fit to inform policy, it is essential to understand and maximize the conditions for the uptake of citizen science by decision-makers to contribute to the locally-relevant and globally-scaled evidence base needed to solve upcoming water challenges.

Source: (OECD, 2019[6]); (OECD, FAO, IIASA, 2020[18])

References

European Parliament (2017), *Nature-based solutions: Concept, opportunities and challenges*, http://www.europarl.europa.eu/thinktank/en/document.html?reference=EPRS_BRI(2017)608796 (accessed on 29 October 2019). [12]

European Union (2000), "EU Water Framework Directive", in *"Directive 2000/60/EC of the European Parliament and of the Council establishing a framework for the Community action in the field of water policy*, European Union, https://eur-lex.europa.eu/legal-content/EN/TXT/?uri=CELEX:32000L0060. [1]

European Union (1991), "EU urban waste-water treatment directive", in *Council Directive concerning urban waste-water treatment*, European Union, https://eur-lex.europa.eu/legal-content/EN/TXT/?uri=CELEX:31991L0271. [3]

Haščič, I. and M. Migotto (2015), "Measuring environmental innovation using patent data", *OECD Environment Working Papers*, No. 89, OECD Publishing, Paris, https://dx.doi.org/10.1787/5js009kf48xw-en. [16]

Leflaive, X., B. Krieble and H. Smythe (2020), "Trends in water-related technological innovation: Insights from patent data", *OECD Environment Working Papers*, No. 161, OECD Publishing, Paris, https://dx.doi.org/10.1787/821c01f2-en. [17]

OECD (2019), *OECD Environmental Performance Reviews: Australia 2019*, OECD Publishing, http://dx.doi.org/10.1787/9789264310452-en. [4]

OECD (2019), *OECD Environmental Performance Reviews: Turkey 2019*, OECD Environmental Performance Reviews, OECD Publishing, Paris, https://dx.doi.org/10.1787/9789264309753-en. [5]

OECD (2019), *OECD workshop on the Implementation of the OECD Council Recommendation on Water. 14 October 2019, Paris.* [6]

OECD (2018), *Implementing the OECD Principles on Water Governance: Indicator Framework and Evolving Practices*, OECD Studies on Water, OECD Publishing, Paris, https://dx.doi.org/10.1787/9789264292659-en. [8]

OECD (2018), *Managing the Water-Energy-Land-Food Nexus in Korea: Policies and Governance Options*, OECD Studies on Water, OECD Publishing, Paris, https://dx.doi.org/10.1787/9789264306523-en. [13]

OECD (2017), *Diffuse Pollution, Degraded Waters: Emerging Policy Solutions*, OECD Studies on Water, OECD Publishing, Paris, https://dx.doi.org/10.1787/9789264269064-en. [11]

OECD (2017), *Enhancing Water Use Efficiency in Korea: Policy Issues and Recommendations*, OECD Studies on Water, OECD Publishing, Paris, https://dx.doi.org/10.1787/9789264281707-en. [2]

OECD (2015), *Drying Wells, Rising Stakes: Towards Sustainable Agricultural Groundwater Use*, OECD Studies on Water, OECD Publishing, Paris, https://dx.doi.org/10.1787/9789264238701-en. [9]

OECD (2015), *Stakeholder Engagement for Inclusive Water Governance*, OECD Studies on Water, OECD Publishing, Paris, https://dx.doi.org/10.1787/9789264231122-en. [10]

OECD (2013), *Water and Climate Change Adaptation: Policies to Navigate Uncharted Waters*, OECD Studies on Water, OECD Publishing, Paris, https://dx.doi.org/10.1787/9789264200449-en. [7]

OECD, FAO, IIASA (2020), *Towards a G20 Action Plan on Water. Background note to the G20 Saudi Presidency.* [18]

Republic of Korea (2020), *Article 21 of the "Framework Act of Water Management". 26 May 2020 (partial amendment)*, Ministry of Government Legislation of the Republic of Korea. [15]

Republic of Korea (2019), *Establishment of Integrated Water Management System, Press Release, 23 January 2019.* [14]

Notes

[1] https://www.eea.europa.eu/data-and-maps/explore-interactive-maps/water-framework-directive-2nd-rbmp

[2] For more information, please visit: https://www.miteco.gob.es/es/agua/temas/planificacion-hidrologica/memoria_infoseg_2018_tcm30-482594.pdf

[3] 2019 OECD Survey on water and agriculture policy changes.

3. Managing water quantity

This chapter presents Adherents' experience with managing water quantity, in line with the OECD Recommendation on Water. The chapter explores how Adherents develop water demand policies by taking into account short and long-term projections and uncertainties while incorporating social, economic and ecological functions. It highlights examples of efforts to promote water use efficiency, the use of economic instruments, water efficient technologies and alternatives sources of water. It also illustrates well-designed water allocation regimes and collective management approaches. Finally, the chapter shares expertise on how knowledge and data support water quantity management.

Water quantity management relies on a combination of policies, at national and sub-national levels of government, to better manage demand for water, promote water use efficiency and allocate water, which varies across seasons and geographically, across uses where it is most needed.[1] The OECD projected that demand for water is set to increase by 55% between 2010 and 2050 globally (Figure 3.1), due to growing demand from manufacturing, energy generation and domestic use (OECD, 2012[1]). There will be increasing competition for water amongst uses and users, putting ecosystems at risk. Groundwater depletion may become the greatest threat to agriculture and urban water supplies in several regions in the coming decades. Climate change will only exacerbate these tensions, as water availability becomes more variable and uncertainty rises about future water availability and demand. The ability to allocate water where it creates most value is a condition for sustainable growth, social equity and environmental performance.

Figure 3.1. Global water demand, 2000-2050

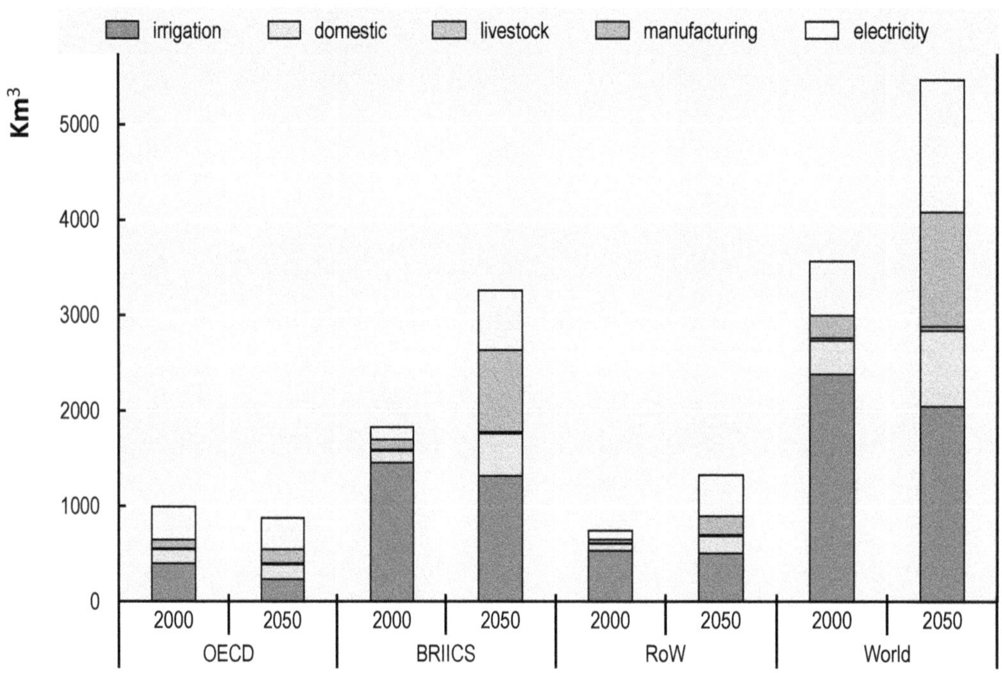

Note: this graph only measures blue water demand and does not consider rain-fed agriculture. RoW refers to Rest of the World.
Source: OECD (2012), *OECD Environmental Outlook to 2050: The Consequences of Inaction*, OECD Publishing, Paris, https://doi.org/10.1787/9789264122246-en.

3.1. Water demand management policies

3.1.1. Short and long term projections and uncertainties

Adherents to the Recommendation are encouraged to manage water quantity through "water demand management policies at national or sub-national levels of government, which reflect short and long-term projections and account for uncertainties on current and future water availability and demand".

A 2012-2013 survey undertaken as part of the work on water and climate change adaptation showed that all Adherent respondents[2] had already observed changes in freshwater systems due to climate change and were conscious of growing uncertainties in water availability and demand (OECD, 2013[2]). Adherents with arid climates, such as **Greece, Israel, Spain, Turkey**, along with Southwest **Australia**, the Northern part of **Chile**, and the Southwest **US**, are especially sensitive to even small changes in precipitation. In **Turkey**, the expected change in the quantity of water, combined with an expected growing demand for water, make the water sector highly vulnerable to the impacts of water scarcity (OECD, 2019[3]). Even Adherents considered relatively water abundant overall, such as **France** or the **Netherlands**, anticipate increased water stress in vulnerable regions due to the impacts of climate change (OECD, 2013[2]).

Several Adherents have made efforts to incorporate uncertainties associated with climate change in their plans and targets. For instance, **Korea's** Ministry of Environment established the Long-Term Comprehensive Plan of Water Resources every 20 years considering climate change explicitly, to be updated every five years. **The Netherlands** has proactively worked to incorporate uncertainty into long-term planning for water management, including the revision of flood protection standards (OECD, 2014[4]). European member states are also required to renew their River Basin Management Plans, outlining objectives on water demand (the latest cycle ran between 2014-20).[3]

However, as of 2015, when the OECD survey on water resources allocation[4] was conducted, less than 60% of survey respondents reported accounting for the potential impacts of climate change in their water resource allocation arrangements, even though doing so is essential to ensure that allocation regimes can cope with changing conditions. Even less common are efforts to review shifting eco-hydrological baselines as climate conditions continue to alter the water cycle (OECD, 2015[5]).[5]

Furthermore, Adherents have focused on better understanding the growing risks related to managing water quantity by building the scientific evidence base and disseminating information (see chapter 5 for more details).

3.1.2. Incorporating social, economic and ecological functions in water quantity management

The Recommendation calls on Adherents to ensure that water demand management policies are "based on water management plans that build upon an understanding of the ecologically sustainable limits of the system, account for all the social, economic and environmental functions of water while preserving water resources. Where needed, water supply can be augmented in sustainable ways, e.g. through modular, scalable approaches to green and grey infrastructure, or the use of reclaimed water."

The importance of environmental flows is widely recognised and many Adherents have reflected their role in their water allocation regimes (OECD, 2015[5]). In the above-mentioned 2015 survey on water resources allocation a majority (76%) of respondents indicated that minimum environmental flows were defined (OECD, 2015[6]). In the 2019 OECD Implementation Survey, 78% of respondents reported that minimum environmental flows/sustainable diversion limits were defined in water allocation mechanisms (Figure 3.2).

Figure 3.2. Environmental flows and sustainable diversion limits in water allocation mechanisms

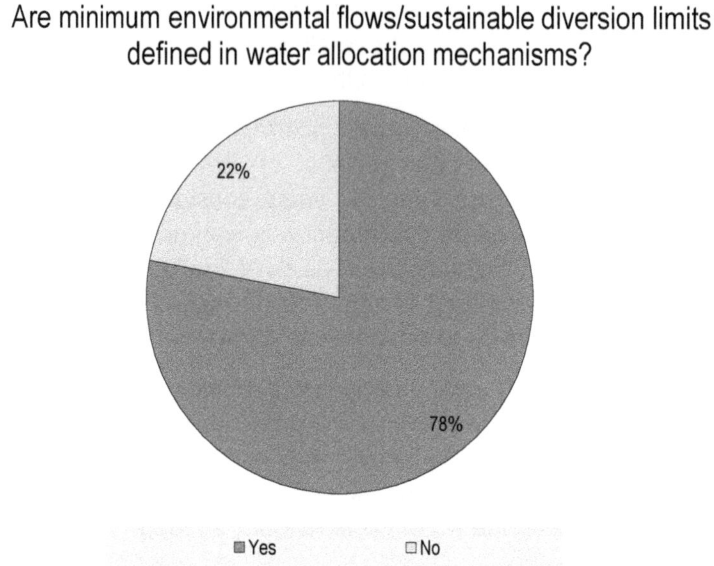

Note: Responses to the question: "Are minimum environmental flows/sustainable diversion limits defined in water allocation mechanisms?". "No" also includes countries that responded "n/a" or "other".
Source: 2019 survey on the implementation of the OECD Council Recommendation on Water; 27 responses received, including 26 Adherents.

The methodologies used to define minimum environmental flows vary. **Israel** sets aside a minimum quota of water for ecosystems in some places. In **Slovenia**, ecologically acceptable flow is based on hydrological, hydro-morphological and biological characteristics of watercourses, features of water abstraction and distinctive protection regimes. England and Wales (**United Kingdom**) use environmental flow indicators. In **Portugal**, minimum environmental flows are determined on a case by case basis. In **France**, the minimum biological flow and the reserve flow required are based on the observation of ecological needs (OECD, 2015[6]). In **Chile** the minimum environmental flows are defined in two ways: they are established by the General Water Directorate (DGA) when allocating new water entitlements and they are defined and included for every major project as part of the required environmental impact assessments.[6] Overall, respondents take into account freshwater and terrestrial biodiversity as part of defining minimum environmental flows (Figure 3.3).

Figure 3.3. Key considerations for defining environmental flows

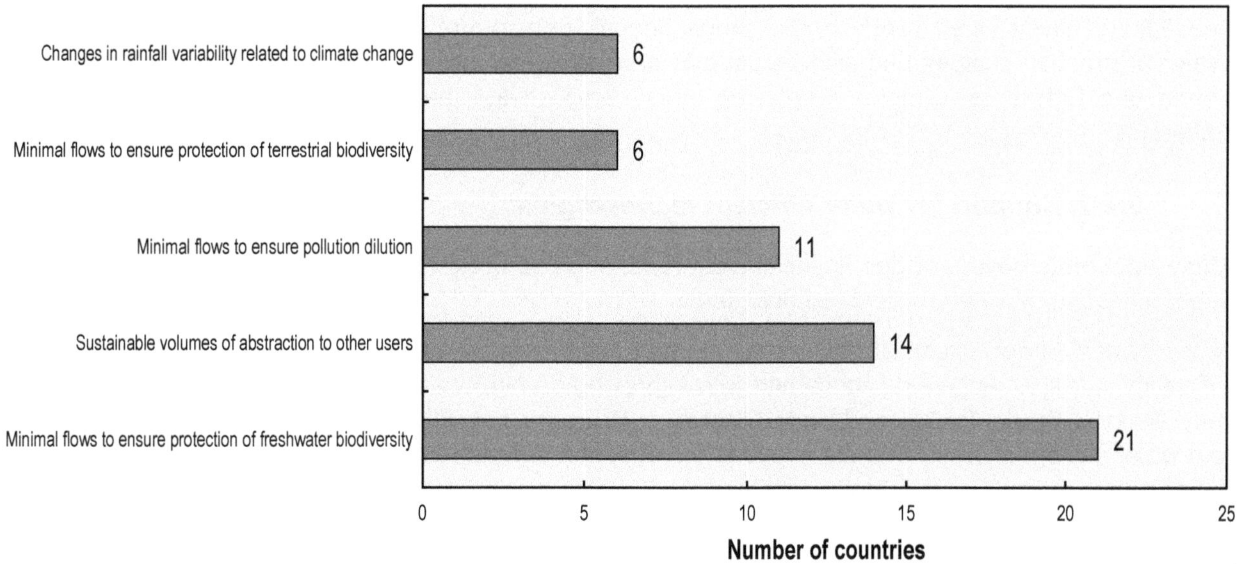

Note: Responses to the question: "Which of the following aspects are taken into account for defining minimum environmental flows/sustainable diversion limits in water allocation mechanisms?". Multiple responses were possible.
Source: 2019 survey on the implementation of the OECD Council Recommendation on Water; 27 responses received, including 26 Adherents.

Ecologically sustainable limits are often, but not always, linked to water management plans. This is the case of the Murray-Darling Basin Plan in **Australia,** which limits water use at environmentally sustainable levels by determining long-term sustainable diversion limits for both surface and groundwater resources. Australian jurisdictions also need to ensure that local environmental flow management and environmental objectives (e.g. on water quality, habitat and pest management) are coherent across complementary waterways (OECD, 2019[7]).

In addition to environmental sustainability, the design of water allocation regimes can incorporate economic efficiency and social equity objectives. To support economically efficient use of water resources, many countries' allocation regimes allow transfer of water entitlements between users, so water can be used for higher value uses. Notable examples include **Australia**, **Chile** and parts of the **United States**. **Israel's** allocation arrangements using differentiated pricing to promote economically efficient allocation among users (OECD, 2015[6]). Chapter 8 outlines more details on countries' water pricing instruments.

3.2. Promoting water use efficiency

Adherents to the Recommendation should manage water quantity through "the promotion of water use efficiency to alleviate pressure on all surface and groundwater resources, especially where water is scarce and competition between sectors intensifies, whilst taking into account the need for groundwater recharge and environmental flows. That promotion can include the consideration of economic instruments for water resources management (e.g. water abstraction charges), support for water-efficient technologies or for the use of alternative sources of water (e.g. reclaimed water)."

3.2.1. Economic instruments

Appropriately designed and locally tailored economic instruments can help allocate water where it is most needed, incentivise its efficient use, and simultaneously generate revenues to manage water resources. Water abstraction charges can also be used to promote water use efficiency, as applied in **Denmark, Latvia** and **Lithuania**. Chapter 7 provides more detail on the use of economic instruments among Adherents.

3.2.2. Support for water efficient technologies

Many Adherents have provided financial incentives, such as tax credits or subsidised interest rates, to support the use of water-efficient technologies.

In the context of agriculture, 28 Adherents reported using farm advice or research to promote water use efficiency in 2019.[7] Adherents concerned with improving on-farm water use efficiency include **Australia, Italy, Mexico, Spain, Turkey and United States**. In **Hungary,** subsidies for irrigation are given conditional to a water saving objective. **France** supports the adoption of water-saving irrigation technologies through subsidised credits for purchasing meters and water saving equipment under its *Plan Végétal Environnement* (OECD, 2010[8]).

Government support for efficient technologies also exist for domestic water use. The previous section reported a series of policies to roll-out smart metering. In New York (**United States**), a reduction on water and sewer charges is given to buildings that maintain a Comprehensive Water Reuse System (CWRS) that can capture, treat and recycle black water (i.e. sanitary wastewater) or grey water (i.e. wastewater from lavatories, showers and clothes washers) (OECD, 2015[9]).

Adherents are also raising awareness of water efficient technologies. For example, Flanders (**Belgium**) set up educational centres to offer trainings for analysing water consumption, informing users about water-saving measures, and carrying out the installation and maintenance works (OECD, 2018[10]).

Caution is required to avoid possible unintended consequences of measures to support water use efficiency, notably in agriculture. There are three risks associated with water efficiency measures in agriculture (OECD, 2016[11]): (i) increased irrigation efficiency can result in increased water consumption and the diminution or elimination of return flows to aquifers or surface water bodies; (ii) farmers taking advantage of more efficient irrigation to switch to more water thirsty activities; and (iii) it can encourage farmers to keep on irrigating activities in the future. The first two effects can lead to a reduction in water availability for other users and the environment and an increased dependence on water resources and the risks associated with climate change (OECD, 2018[12]; OECD, 2016[11]). Water allocation regimes should account for the return flows of water abstracted through entitlements, otherwise, increased use efficiency can reduce overall water availability in the system (OECD, 2015[6]). This is a challenge found in **Australia's** Murray Darling Basin where the national government and states and territories have worked hard to improve water provision for the environment through water plans and by acquiring entitlements. Water markets have helped deliver environmental outcomes through the purchase of water for the environment (e.g. about 20% of water entitlements in the Murray Darling Basin is managed for the environment). Yet there have been concerns about the appropriation of environmental flows in the state of New South Wales (Gruère, Ashley and Cadilhon, 2018[13]). Continued improvement in monitoring and reporting of water managed to deliver environmental benefits is important to help build public trust in water management and make best use of environmental water (OECD, 2019[7]). Indeed, appropriate water accounting at the basin scale that considers not just withdrawals but also water returning to the system is a first step for mitigating these unintended consequences of water use efficiency gains.

To cope with this issue, a number of Adherents have set conditions on water efficiency investments or the delivery of water entitlements to ensure water sustainability. European Union member states, like **Denmark, Greece** or **Hungary**, deliver groundwater permits only under condition that it does not affect the ecological status of water resources. **Italy** discourages investment in irrigation infrastructure, like impermeable canals, in area where groundwater recharge is needed.[8]

3.2.3. Alternative sources of water

Tapping into alternative water sources, such as rain and storm water, used water[9], and desalinated sea or brackish water, can help alleviate water scarcity. Reused water, supplied from either centralised or decentralised distributed systems, is increasingly seen as a sustainable source for some uses of water, such as for irrigation, groundwater recharge, and possibly for non-potable domestic uses.

The **European Union** has just approved its regulation on minimum requirements for water reuse for irrigation. **Spain** has a water reuse regulation in force since 2007 and several reclaimed water plants operate in the east part of the country and the Canary and Balearic Islands[10]. The city of Barcelona (**Spain**), for example, manages three reclaimed water plants (OECD, 2015[9]). **Spain** is also implementing a National Plan of Water Treatment, Sanitation, Efficiency, Savings and Water Reuse (DSEAR Plan), which promotes and increases the use of reuse water. **Israel** is the largest user of recycled effluent water for agricultural and has increased freshwater prices for farmers to encourage this recycled water (OECD, 2015[6]). In **Australia**, wastewater recycling, desalination and storm water harvesting and reuse are increasingly part of the portfolio of best practices for providing and maintaining water supplies. In the city of Perth (**Australia**), desalination is the primary water source, contributing 48% of its potable drinking water supplies followed by groundwater (40%), dams (10%) and groundwater replenishment (2%).

Health-related risks (e.g. possible water contamination during domestic use, or salinisation of irrigated soils) need to be taken into consideration in the development of alternative sources of water. The National Water Quality Management Strategy in **Australia**, for example, addresses such risks by including quality guidelines and monitoring for the safe use of recycled water. The level of standards for reused water can influence the payback period of the additional investment costs required (e.g. equipment, or in-house dual plumbing) (OECD, 2009[14]).

3.3. Water allocation regimes

The Recommendation encourages Adherents to manage water quantity through "water allocation regimes that define a sustainable resource pool". These regimes are a combination of policies, laws and mechanisms to help determine who is able to use water resources, how, when and where. The Recommendation develops ways to strengthen water allocation:

The Recommendation calls for "allocat[ing] water and the risk of shortage in a manner that is non-discriminatory and that reflects wider policy objectives (e.g. access to drinking water, ecosystems health, food or energy security), under both average and extreme conditions, including through balancing all interests in basins and considering the cost-effectiveness of measures". In the Recommendation, water allocation refers to the national parts of rivers, lakes and aquifers.

The 2015 water allocation survey documented that allocation regimes can exist at different scales within national contexts: some are set at national level (e.g. **Costa Rica, Estonia, Luxembourg, Slovenia, Switzerland**), others at province/state level (e.g. **Canada**, **Brazil**), or at river basin scale (e.g. **Australia, Colombia, Spain**). Allocation regimes may differ for surface and ground water systems (e.g. **Austria**). The 2015 survey also showed that in times of scarcity most allocation regimes have an established sequence of priority uses to determine which sectors or uses will be allocated available water prior to others (Figure 3.4). Unsurprisingly, domestic and human needs often rank as the highest priority (e.g. **Australia**, **Brazil**, **Colombia, Israel, Portugal**) (OECD, 2015[6]).

Box 3.1. Water allocation systems at a River Basin District level in Spain

Spain's 25 river basin management plans cover the allocation and reservation of water resources - water distributions within each district - with the aim of meeting water needs for current and future uses. This information is critical not only for dealing with the socio-economic aspects, but also for assessing the impact produced by it, calculating accurately the environmental objectives in water bodies and, as the case might be, rationalising the application of exemptions to the compliance of such objectives.

The allocation and reservation of resources available for the foreseeable demands has been carried out based on the results of the balance obtained for the demands scenario established for the year 2021. Likewise, river basin management plans have listed those demands which cannot be met with the resources available within the corresponding river basin districts. The allocation and reservation of resources is considered a key measure by Spain to address the water scarcity and manage water abstractions.

Source: country contribution

Most allocation regimes impose an overall limit ("cap") on water that can be abstracted from a resource pool; although in practice this limit may not be respected (OECD, 2015[6]). There is variation in terms of how that cap is defined. A large majority of respondents surveyed put a limit on the *volume* of water that can be abstracted (57%), some put a limit on the *share* of water that can be abstracted (14%), while some others restrict *who can abstract* water, but without limit on how much water can be abstracted (11%) (OECD, 2015[6]). For groundwater, setting an abstraction limit requires consideration of the amount of water that should be left in the aquifer to meet non-extractive uses (e.g. flows for ecosystem needs, protection of water quality) and future uses. Examples from **Denmark**, **Mexico**, **United States** (Texas) and **France** illustrate approaches to limit the long-term abstraction of groundwater (OECD, 2017[15]).

The Recommendation also encourages Adherents to ensure that water allocation regimes "are dynamic, flexible and adjusted to shifting circumstances at the least social cost". Flexibility can be delivered through the design of regulations (e.g. unbundling of abstraction licencing arrangements from land titles in **Australia** and most other Adherents particularly for surface water) or in the design of the cap (a proportional cap as a share of available water, rather than a fixed volume). Further, many Adherents (i.e. two-thirds of allocation regimes surveyed in 2015) allow for water entitlements to be traded, leased or transferred, under specific conditions and with approval of the responsible authority, to provide an incentive for efficient water use and innovation. This occurs in formalised water markets such as in **Australia** (Murray-Darling Basin), **Chile** or **Spain**. It can also take place with an abstraction licensing system such as in the **United Kingdom**.

Figure 3.4. Sequence of priority uses in water allocation among selected Adherents

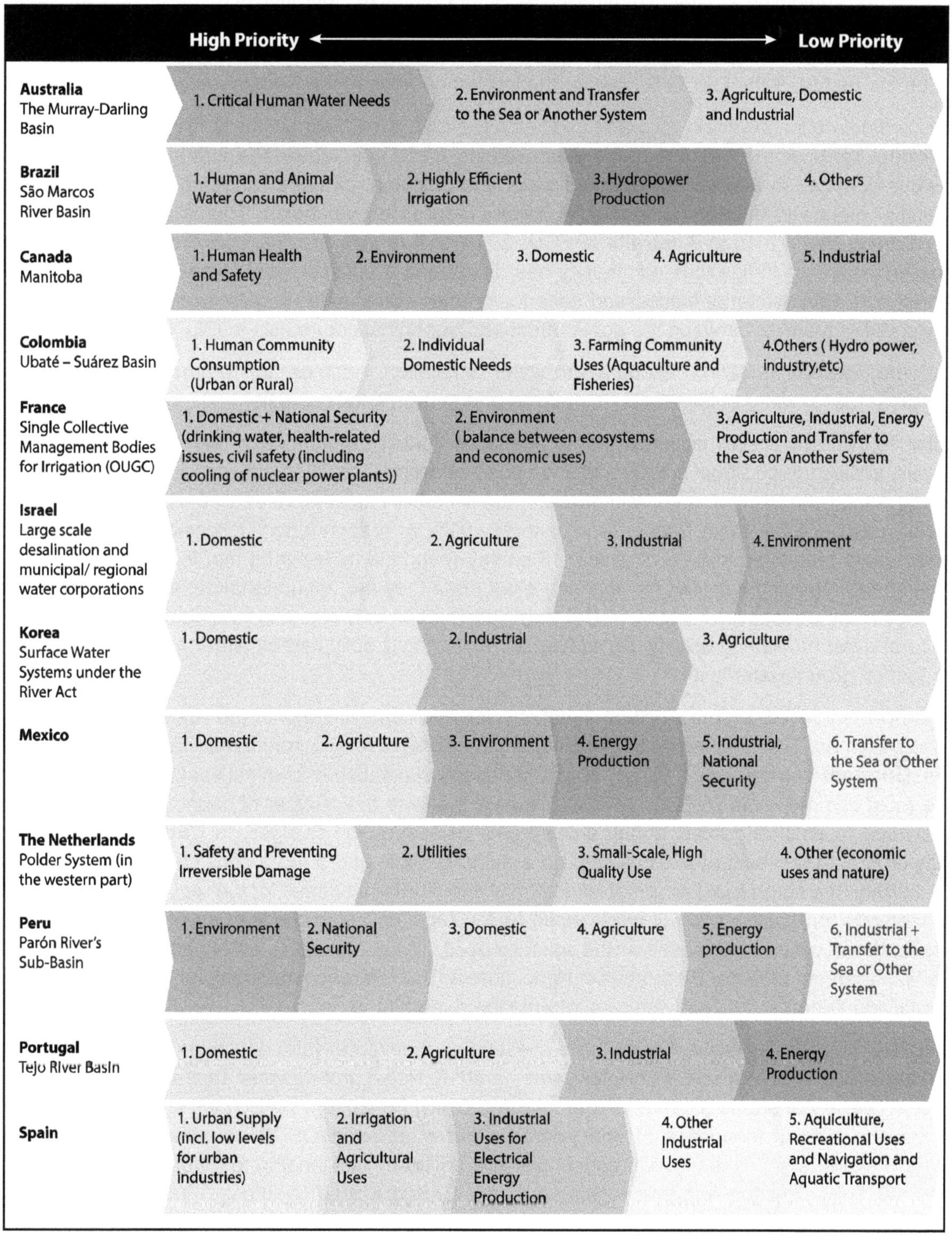

Note: More examples available in country profiles at www.oecd.org/environment/water-resources-allocation-9789264229631-en.htm.
Source: (OECD, 2015[16])

Furthermore, the Recommendation calls for water allocation regimes to "promote efficient water use, investment and innovation, with due regard for social consequences and the ecosystem-support function of water". This requires an allocation regime that provides incentives for efficient resource use and removes perverse incentives for inefficient use. This can be done through appropriate abstraction charges or fees, a key part of allocation regimes. Chapter 7 provides an overview of the adoption of abstraction charges based on the results of the OECD Survey on the Implementation of the Recommendation on Water.

The Recommendation also calls for water allocation regimes to be "responsive to the customary practices of traditional communities". Where these exist, valuing traditional knowledge through the recognition of indigenous peoples' stewardship of land and water and customary water arrangements can potentially be an effective means to enhance sustainable development in a river basin. This is a component of the Murray-Darling Basin Plan in **Australia** (OECD, 2019[7]). It is also prevalent for the Fitzroy River basin (**Australia**) where an indigenous community has developed a political declaration aiming to protect the traditional and environmental values and calls for greater stakeholder engagement and ultimately joint management of the river between the government and aboriginal communities (OECD, 2018[10]).

Finally, the Recommendation encourages water allocation regimes to "promote compliance and enforcement (i.e. of water entitlements) in national and sub-national contexts".

Compliance systems are an essential tool to strengthen public confidence in the management of water resources, to discourage illegal activity and drive positive action. The 2015 water allocation survey showed that most Adherents monitor water withdrawals and enforce allocation rules in their allocation regimes. Industrial users are the most frequently monitored (91% of respondents), followed by agriculture and domestic users monitored in 88% of cases. 18 survey respondents reported that they conduct metering, monitoring and reporting activities for agriculture but often they are not undertaken nationally but in areas where significant abstractions occur. In **Belgium**, declaration of water consumption is necessary as an agricultural water monitoring activity. An additional monitoring is obligated for larger abstractions to assess the impact on groundwater level. [11]

Two-thirds of surveyed regimes include sanctions for non-compliance with the rules and regulations of allocation regimes. With the introduction of statutory instruments for Environmental Civil Sanctions in 2010, **United Kingdom** can now use a variety of civil sanctions in addition to criminal sanctions. Monetary fines are the most common type (OECD, 2015[6]). Figure 3.5 shows the number of countries that use different data sources to enforce quotas, rights, entitlements or abstraction charges. In **Cabo Verde**, the water quantity control for agriculture is conducted on a monthly basis and a more consistent database is being set up. In **Italy**, the Ministerial Decree of Ministry of Agriculture "guidelines for the regulation by the regions of the methods for quantification of water volumes for irrigation", promote the use of water metering and the application of water prices based on the volumes used. The guidelines use National Information System for the Management of Water Resources in Agriculture as the reference database for the collection of data for quantifying irrigation volumes and also information related to permits.

Groundwater specificities make it much more challenging to enforce water allocation systems, particularly in rural areas with a large number of water users. In 2019, illegal groundwater abstractions were reported to occur in twelve Adherents (Gruère, Shigemitsu and Crawford, 2020[17]). Also past studies estimated that there may be tens of thousands of unregulated wells in selected OECD countries (OECD, 2015[18]). Metering of wells is not systematic in agriculture and politically challenging to introduce (Gruère and Le Boëdec, 2019[19]). To cope with this, regulators in the **United States** (Nebraska) have encouraged self-metering by farmers, which has proven to induce positive results, and other Adherents have used indirect measures, such as metering energy use or the estimation of water consumption with remote sensing data.

3.4. Collective management approaches

The Recommendation promotes collective management approaches - defined as collective entitlements – where applicable, in areas "where little information is available on water availability and use, or where the transaction costs of managing individual entitlements are too high (e.g. for groundwater management)". This is particularly important for groundwater management, where aquifers can operate as common resource pools (OECD, 2015[18]).

Collective management is widely used in the management of irrigation. Water user associations or irrigators groups are operating in **Japan, Korea**, and **EU** member states (like **Estonia, Sweden** or **Portugal**). In the **United Kingdom**, water abstractor groups have the potential to share abstraction licences to effectively manage water resources in a more efficient and sustainable manner. Examples of self-regulated groundwater management in the states of Kansas and Colorado in the **United States** show that this mechanism can be effective. [12]

France institutionalised collective management bodies, the *organismes uniques de gestion collective* (OUGCs), whose role is to provide a structure and incentives for irrigators to devise their own rules to allocate a set volume of water among themselves at the catchment level. However, some challenges emerged with their implementation due to the conflictual relations between those exercising the tasks of the OUGCs and those who are meant to benefit from them (OECD, 2017[15]). In **Costa Rica**, the Ministry of Energy and Environment grants water abstraction permits (called concessions) to an entity that has the authority to decide internally on the form of water distribution amongst their members. They are required for surface water or groundwater uptake (Gruère and Le Boëdec, 2019[20]).

3.5. Improved knowledge and data

Adherents to the Recommendation are encouraged to manage water quantity through "improved knowledge of water use and sustainability limits, and improved monitoring of water resources and uses, watershed conditions, ecosystems health and the interconnections between surface and groundwater, to better assess environmental needs and future water availability and make more robust decisions."

All Adherents monitor their water resources and uses *to a certain extent* to help understand how much water can be used for varied and competing demands, while still preserving water resources on which many social, economic and environmental functions rely. Figure 3.5 shows the different data sources used to facilitate water quantity management by respondents, whereby reporting obligations as well as in-situ monitoring by public authorities remain the most frequently used sources for collecting monitoring data.

Figure 3.5. Data sources to facilitate water quantity management

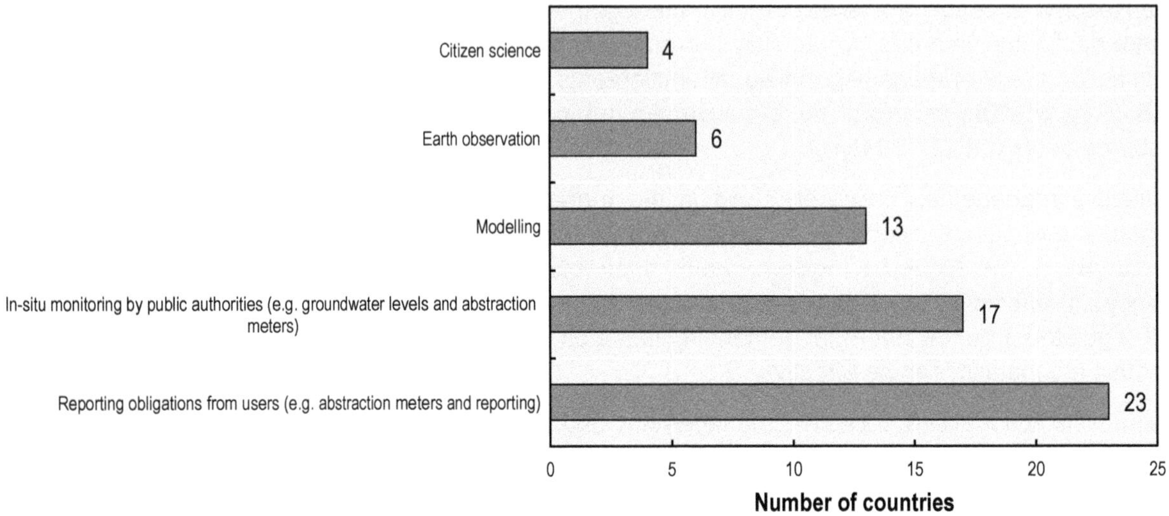

Note: Responses to the question: "What data sources are used to facilitate enforcement of water quantity management (e.g. quotas, rights, or entitlements or abstraction charges)?". Multiple responses were possible. The US Environment Protection Agency does not regulate water quantity and therefore did not respond to this question.
Source: 2019 survey on the implementation of the OECD Council Recommendation on Water; 27 responses received, including 26 Adherents.

There have been efforts across OECD to improve mapping of surface and groundwater. This has been done using innovative data sources such as earth observation data (see further details in General water policy, chapter 2). Good information should be collected on local contexts and the dominant drivers (and their projected impact) on groundwater resources in the future. Such information needs to be converted into knowledge in order to enable public authorities and stakeholders to take informed management decisions; develop effective rights and allocation regimes; prevent conflicts; and protect and groundwater quality in the long term (Akhmouch, 2017[21]). For instance, the **United States** NASA's Gravity Recovery and Climate Experiment (GRACE) was the first satellite mission of its kind to changes in these groundwater resources over time (OECD, 2017[15]). A mapping exercise has been undertaken in **France** to identify ground and surface water stressed areas and defines zones where policies aim to restore sustainable volumes of water abstraction (OECD, 2015[6]). The water information system is under development in **Turkey** is to gather data, maps, statistics and policy documents, and is to be based on a spatial mapping tool to improve data visualisation and make the system more user-friendly to the broader public (OECD, 2018[10]). Many challenges remain in monitoring the use and sustainability of water uses. For example, it remains difficult to monitor aquifers because it is technically demanding and costly (OECD, 2017[15]). Well metering requirements are only a recent development (see above) and therefore groundwater markets may be more difficult to establish than surface water markets (OECD, 2019[3]).

References

Akhmouch, A. (2017), *Assessing and monitoring groundwater governance*, https://doi.org/10.1201/9781315210025. [21]

Gruère, G., C. Ashley and J. Cadilhon (2018), "Reforming water policies in agriculture: Lessons from past reforms", *OECD Food, Agriculture and Fisheries Papers*, No. 113, OECD Publishing, Paris, https://dx.doi.org/10.1787/1826beee-en. [13]

Gruère, G. and H. Le Boëdec (2019), "Navigating pathways to reform water policies in agriculture", *OECD Food, Agriculture and Fisheries Papers*, No. 128, OECD Publishing, Paris, https://dx.doi.org/10.1787/906cea2b-en. [19]

Gruère, G. and H. Le Boëdec (2019), "Navigating pathways to reform water policies in agriculture", *OECD Food, Agriculture and Fisheries Papers*, No. 128, OECD Publishing, Paris, https://dx.doi.org/10.1787/906cea2b-en. [20]

Gruère, G., M. Shigemitsu and S. Crawford (2020), "Agriculture and water policy changes: Stocktaking and alignment with OECD and G20 recommendations", *OECD Food, Agriculture and Fisheries Papers*, No. 144, OECD Publishing, Paris, https://dx.doi.org/10.1787/f35e64af-en. [17]

OECD (2019), *OECD Environmental Performance Reviews: Australia 2019*, OECD Publishing, http://dx.doi.org/10.1787/9789264310452-en. [7]

OECD (2019), *OECD Environmental Performance Reviews: Turkey 2019*, OECD Environmental Performance Reviews, OECD Publishing, Paris, https://dx.doi.org/10.1787/9789264309753-en. [3]

OECD (2018), *Implementing the OECD Principles on Water Governance: Indicator Framework and Evolving Practices*, OECD Studies on Water, OECD Publishing, Paris, https://dx.doi.org/10.1787/9789264292659-en. [10]

OECD (2018), *Managing the Water-Energy-Land-Food Nexus in Korea: Policies and Governance Options*, OECD Studies on Water, OECD Publishing, Paris, https://dx.doi.org/10.1787/9789264306523-en. [12]

OECD (2017), *Groundwater Allocation: Managing Growing Pressures on Quantity and Quality*, OECD Studies on Water, OECD Publishing, Paris, https://dx.doi.org/10.1787/9789264281554-en. [15]

OECD (2016), *Mitigating Droughts and Floods in Agriculture: Policy Lessons and Approaches*, OECD Studies on Water, OECD Publishing, Paris, https://dx.doi.org/10.1787/9789264246744-en. [11]

OECD (2015), *Drying Wells, Rising Stakes: Towards Sustainable Agricultural Groundwater Use*, OECD Studies on Water, OECD Publishing, Paris, https://dx.doi.org/10.1787/9789264238701-en. [18]

OECD (2015), *Water and Cities: Ensuring Sustainable Futures*, OECD Studies on Water, OECD Publishing, Paris, https://dx.doi.org/10.1787/9789264230149-en. [9]

OECD (2015), *Water Resources Allocation*, http://www.oecd.org/environment/resources/Water-Resources-Allocation-Policy-Highlights-web.pdf. [16]

OECD (2015), *Water Resources Allocation: Sharing Risks and Opportunities*, OECD Studies on Water, OECD Publishing, Paris, https://dx.doi.org/10.1787/9789264229631-en. [6]

OECD (2015), *Water Resources Governance in Brazil*, OECD Studies on Water, OECD Publishing, Paris, https://dx.doi.org/10.1787/9789264238121-en. [5]

OECD (2014), *Water Governance in the Netherlands: Fit for the Future?*, OECD Studies on Water, OECD Publishing, Paris, https://dx.doi.org/10.1787/9789264102637-en. [4]

OECD (2013), *Water and Climate Change Adaptation: Policies to Navigate Uncharted Waters*, OECD Studies on Water, OECD Publishing, Paris, https://dx.doi.org/10.1787/9789264200449-en. [2]

OECD (2012), *OECD Environmental Outlook to 2050: The Consequences of Inaction*, OECD Publishing, Paris, https://dx.doi.org/10.1787/9789264122246-en. [1]

OECD (2010), *Sustainable Management of Water Resources in Agriculture*, OECD Studies on Water, OECD Publishing, Paris, https://dx.doi.org/10.1787/9789264083578-en. [8]

OECD (2009), *Alternative Ways of Providing Water: Emerging Options and their Policy Implications*, OECD Publishing, http://www.oecd.org/env/resources/42349741.pdf. [14]

Notes

[1] In the Recommendation, water allocation refers to the national parts of rivers, lakes and aquifers.

[2] Survey answers were received from all Adherents that were OECD members at the time of the report in 2013, plus the European Commission.

[3] 2019 OECD Survey on water and agriculture policy changes.

[4] The OECD survey covered 27 OECD and key partner countries, documenting 37 distinct water allocation regimes. For further details, see (OECD, 2015[6]).

[5] Moreover, the 2019 OECD Survey on water and agriculture policy changes showed that only 41% of Adherents that set quantified national planning targets for the use of water resources in the agriculture sector (sixteen Adherents), account for climate change.

[6] 2019 OECD Survey on water and agriculture policy changes.

[7] 2019 OECD Survey on water and agriculture policy changes.

[8] 2019 OECD Survey on water and agriculture policy changes.

[9] Reused water (either reclaimed water or grey water from wastewater from domestic uses such as laundry, dishwashing, or bathing)

[10] Royal Decree 1620/2007: https://www.boe.es/buscar/pdf/2007/BOE-A-2007-21092-consolidado.pdf

[11] 2019 OECD Survey on water and agriculture policy changes.

[12] 2019 OECD Survey on water and agriculture policy changes.

4. Improving water quality

This chapter represents progress made by Adherents on improving water quality, in line with the OECD Recommendation on Water. The chapter focuses on Adherents' efforts to allocate adequate resources to manage water pollution. It reviews risk mitigation and water reduction pollution strategies as well as Adherents' efforts to select cost-effectiveness solutions and apply the polluter pays principle. It also explores compliance with regulatory provisions and Adherent's efforts to promote sustainable use of water-related ecosystems. Finally, the chapter focuses on ensuring coherence water and sectoral policies.

Policies for improving water quality aim to protect, restore and promote sustainable use of surface, groundwater and coastal ecosystems, halt and reverse degradation, and halt biodiversity loss. They aim to reduce, to the extent necessary, the pollution of all waters from both diffuse and point sources of pollution. The Recommendation calls upon Adherents "to prevent, reduce and manage water pollution, from all sources (diffuse and point sources), in surface and ground waters and related coastal ecosystems, while paying attention to pollutants of emerging concern".

4.1. Allocation of resources to manage water pollution

The Recommendation suggests Adherents "allocate adequate human, technical, scientific and financial resources to assess water and effluent quantity and quality. Water quality monitoring should be developed and publicly reported".

The **EU** Water Framework Directive requires that countries monitor in each river basin district the status of surface water, groundwater and protected areas. Article 8 specifically requires that monitoring programmes for water status are set up to monitor the ecological and chemical status of surface waters and the chemical status of groundwater. This enables to assess water conditions, for example in **Lithuania**, where a majority of surface water bodies are in good chemical and ecological status and all groundwater bodies are in good chemical and quantitative status, all main sources of pollution are identified, and their pollution loads quantified (OECD, 2017[1]).

There are a range of parameters that need to be monitored because of their impact on the environment and risk to human health. In **Korea**, the Integrated Groundwater Information Service supports the mapping of groundwater level and quality data across Korea. Countries are also monitoring aquatic invertebrates, plants and fish. For instance, the National Aquatic Ecological Monitoring Programme monitors ecosystems at 3 880 spots nationwide including main streams of the four major Korean rivers as well as tributaries, small rivers, etc.

A combination of approaches are used in some Adherents to monitor water quality of different nature at different scale. For instance **Ireland** includes national modelling tools and maps, national programmes that are defined at local level to respond to its requirements under the Water Framework Directive and Agriculture Catchment Programmes to monitor nutrient run-offs. The **United Kingdom** applies chemical and ecological monitoring methods, remote sensing models, water quality models, catchment specific methods, sediment finger printing approaches and even citizen based reporting (WaterBlitz).[1]

Contaminants of emerging concern (CECs) are considered so because they have only recently appeared in water, or are of recent concern due to concentration levels higher than expected, or their risk to human and environmental health may not be fully understood.[2] While there is good progress among Adherents in establishing watch-lists and voluntary monitoring programmes for certain pharmaceuticals in surface water, the majority of active pharmaceuticals ingredients, metabolites and transformation products remain unmonitored. Countries are thus increasingly making efforts to identify pollutants of emerging concerns, such is the case of Switzerland (Box 4.1).

Box 4.1. Identifying and prioritising indicator substances for contaminant of emerging concerns monitoring in Switzerland

Switzerland has prioritised five indicator substances to reduce analytical costs of monitoring for an extensive list of contaminant of emerging concerns. Out of a total of 250 substances (pharmaceuticals, pesticide and transformation products) identified in Swiss rivers, 47 indicator substances were identified through a selection process based on five criteria: i) partitioning of substances between water and solid phase; ii) persistence in the aquatic environment; iii) toxicity; iv) concentration patterns (continuous, periodic or intermittent); and v) probability of detecting a substance in surface waters.

To reduce the analytical costs for monitoring all 47 compounds, a subgroup of five indicator compounds was identified to be included in sampling programmes: carbamazepine (anticonvulsant or anti-epileptic drug), diclofenac (nonsteroidal anti-inflammatory drug), sulfamethoxazole (antibiotic), mecoprop (herbicide) and benzotriazole (anticorrosive agent). All of these substances can be measured with the same analytical method and are detectable in more than 90 % of all domestic wastewater treatment effluents in Switzerland.

Source: (OECD, 2019[2]) using Götz, Kase and Hollender, 2011

Remote sensing and imaging technologies such as satellites and drones are becoming key elements to managing water resources at service area, watershed and regional scales. These technologies provide data for mapping water resources, measuring water levels and quality, and utility asset management. Data from such technologies can better prepare water resource managers and utilities for incidences of heavy storm water flow (e.g., altering operations to prevent sewage overflow), indicate when conservation practices should be activated during periods of drought (e.g., reducing water use, use of emergency wells), ensure all treated water is delivered to customers, and provide water quality data (e.g., turbidity, algal blooms) (OECD, FAO, IIASA, 2020[3]).

Water quality monitoring results are best shared with the public through report cards (e.g. Great Barrier Reef Report Card in **Australia**) or as part of wider reporting process on the state of the environment (OECD, 2019[4]). Many jurisdictions also developed dedicated digital content for making data available to a very wide audience. For instance, the Seoul Metropolitan government (**Korea**) works on water quality through an online monitoring system for water quality (OECD, 2015[5]). **Italy** uses an Information System for the Protection of Water (SINTAI), an open source dataset available on line inventorying pollution releases from diffuse sources at the national level, using data from regional sources (OECD, 2013[6]).

The Water Recommendation further suggests to use resources to "identify sources of pollution (diffuse and point sources), and for the most relevant pollutants, assess the concentrations, total amounts and timing of discharges".

Pollution from point sources is largely under control among many Adherents (OECD, 2017[7]). In **Australia**, for instance, the main types of point-source pollution, which are discharges from municipal treatment plants and industrial facilities, do no longer significantly affect the water environment (OECD, 2019[4]). In **Korea**, point source pollution control improved drastically thanks to the expansion in wastewater treatment services, including with tertiary wastewater treatment (OECD, 2018[8]). The **EU** Urban Wastewater Directive, focussing on pollution at source, helps protects the water environment from adverse effects of discharges of urban waste water and from certain industrial discharges.

Adherents still face challenges when it comes to monitoring diffuse pollution and its impacts on human and ecosystem health, which largely remain under-reported and under-regulated (OECD, 2017[7]). These are particularly prevalent in the agriculture sector. Figure 4.1 shows the main pollutants from agriculture sector as reported by Adherents responding to the OECD Survey on water and agriculture policy changes 2019.

[3] Almost all these Adherents identify nitrates and phosphorus from mineral fertilisers as well as animal waste as the most problematic source of agriculture pollution of water. Pesticides from agriculture also remain an important pollutant in many responding countries (Figure 4.1). Under the Clean Water Act, each state in the **United States** is tasked with developing Total Maximum Daily Load (TMDL) allocations specifying allowable loads of nutrients and sediment into impaired waters. Although TMDLs for agriculture serve as overall targets for appropriate loads, pollution from agricultural sources is not directly regulated at a national level and therefore enforcement is achieved through indirect means such as more stringent regulation of point sources.

Figure 4.1. Key pollutants of concern coming from the agricultural sector

Number of countries listing a particular type of pollutant

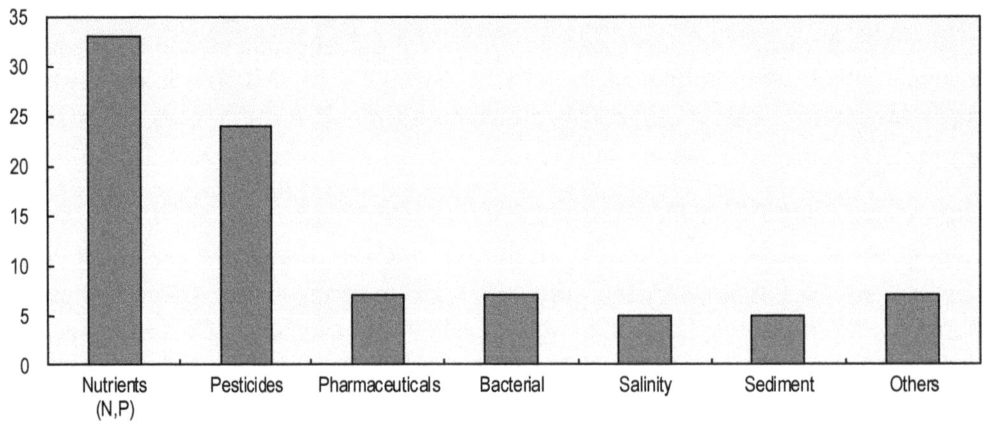

Source: (Gruère, Shigemitsu and Crawford, 2020[9]).

The use of information and communication technologies, by helping to fill some of the water-related information gaps, can usefully inform water-related policies and practices. Countries are using sensor technology for real-time monitoring, satellite imagery and data processing and modelling capabilities to support their water quality monitoring and controlling efforts. **New Zealand** uses the national farm-scale nutrient budgeting and loss estimation model to manage its diffuse pollution outputs (Box 4.2). **Denmark** also uses sophisticated tools to estimate the flows of nutrient pollution and implement spatially differentiated regulations (Gruère and Le Boëdec, 2019[10]).

Box 4.2. Nutrient modelling in New Zealand

OVERSEER®, a national model for farm-scale nutrient budgeting and loss estimation, calculates nutrient flows in a productive farming system and identifies risks of environmental impacts through nutrient loss, including run-off and leaching. The model was originally developed as a tool for farming to create nutrient budgets and has been adapted to overcome barriers that arise from an inability to clearly identify diffuse source polluters. It is recognised as the best tool currently available for estimating nitrate leaching losses from the root zone across the diversity and complexity of farming systems in New Zealand.

OVERSEER® can, and has, supported environmental policy development, most notably around Lake Taupō and as part of Horizons One Plan in the Manawatū-Wānganui region. New Zealand farmers will increasingly use the model to develop nutrient management plans and budgets, as required by regional councils. While such a model is essential for enabling a water pollution cap to be imposed, it is accepted by both farmers and regional councils that it has high uncertainties. The model is not designed to provide economic analysis, so outputs need to be combined with other economic models to assess the impacts of options on the farm business.

Source: (OECD, 2017[11]); (OECD, 2017[7])

The Recommendation further recommends to use resources to "set policy objectives and targets to achieve and maintain assigned water quality standards in water bodies, in order to protect designated uses and water-related ecosystems, taking into account water quality requirements for all water uses". It also calls for improving "standards for water quality target setting, building on the latest scientific knowledge and the most cost-effective technologies".

Water policy objectives are defined to protect designated uses and water-related ecosystems. The **EU** Water Framework Directive defines five levels for the ecological status of surface water bodies: "high", "good", "moderate", "poor" and "bad" according to a combination of biological quality elements (aquatic flora, benthic invertebrate fauna and fish fauna) and physico-chemical quality elements (such as oxygenation conditions, nutrient conditions, salinity, as well as specific pollutants). Other parameters such as microbiological or morphological can be taken into account.

There are different levels of water quality desired for identified uses such as drinking, recreation, farming, fish production, propagation of other aquatic life, and agricultural and industrial processes. These uses might need undisturbed water quality (e.g. ecosystem functioning), defined water quality standards (e.g. drinking water) or might not need water quality standards (e.g. extraction of minerals). The **EU** Directives include explicit quality standards for surface waters (e.g. Directive for abstraction of drinking water, 75/440/EEC) while other Directives, although generally aiming at improvement of surface water and groundwater, do not contain explicit water quality standards (e.g. the Urban Wastewater Directive 91/271/EEC or the Nitrate Directive 91/676/EEC).

Countries are using different methods to set standards. For instance in **New Zealand** the Collaborative Governance Model supports the definition of water quality limits (Box 4.3). **Chile** has adopted standards for sewerage discharges, as well as water quality standards for ecosystem protection for four river basins and two lake catchments which provide water to major cities. In **Korea**, the total pollution load management (TPLM) system, introduced in 2004, helped improve water quality management policy and reduce point source pollution. The TPLM are calculated using scientific water quality modelling at the watershed, local and individual property levels. It allocates pollution load reductions necessary to reduce the sources of pollution (OECD, 2017[7]).

Box 4.3. The collaborative governance model of the Canterbury Water Management Strategy (CWMS), New Zealand

The river basin committee, together with the local community and technical support (with expertise in economics, cultural values, social science, modelling, water quality and ecology), developed a water quality implementation programme comprising of: i) desired community water quality outcomes; ii) recommendations for water quality limits based on maintaining the trophic state of a significant regional lake; iii) catchment nutrient loads for all activities; iv) the method of allocating the nutrient loads; v) methods to incentivise biodiversity protection; vi) non-statutory actions such as an education campaign for visitors; vii) a rehabilitation programme for degraded water bodies; and viii) an integrated monitoring framework for the committee to track progress and to share data.

The Collaborative Governance Model not only resolved how to set water quality (and quantity) limits and other actions to deliver on the CWMS targets, but also facilitated delivering on the National Policy Statement for Freshwater Management. One of the most tangible outcomes was community ownership of solutions.

Source: (OECD, 2018[8])

Finally, the Recommendation suggests Adherents to use resources to "Assess the investments necessary to achieve the desired level of water quality and to protect and restore water-related ecosystems, taking account of cost-effectiveness related to human and ecosystem health benefits".

Investment in water supply and sanitation services typically generates a number of economic, environmental and social benefits. Benefits from the provision of basic water supply and sanitation services have been reaped in the late 19th or early 20th century in most Adherent countries, with now a marginal rate of return of water and sanitation interventions that diminishes with the increasing sophistication of measures. In contrast, relatively high cost investments required in wastewater treatment have benefits, through the removal of different polluting substances (generating benefits for municipal water supply as much as for fishing), which are more difficult to assess in monetary terms. In the **United States**, the 1972 Clean Water Act built an important legal basis for expanding wastewater treatment facilities. The 1991 **EU** Urban Waste Water Treatment Directive (UWWTD) addressed to the growing problem of untreated sewage disposed into the aquatic environment (OECD, 2011[12]).

In a recent collaboration with the European Commission, the OECD projected that all EU member states will need to increase the current level of investments in wastewater collection and treatment by 20% or more, to reach (or preserve) compliance with the UWWTD. Some countries will need to more than double current level of spending. (OECD, 2020).

One reason why investments in water quality lag behind in most Adherent countries is that the benefits they generate are often insufficiently documented. Investing in water supply and sanitation for improved water quality can bring a wide range of benefits to the economy. For instance, the health benefits of quality improvements of recreational waters in south-west Scotland (**United Kingdom**) have been calculated at GBP 1.3 billion per year. In most countries, access to beaches or lakes can be limited in cases of non-compliance with certain bathing norms. In Normandy (**France**), it has been estimated that closing 40% of the coastal beaches would lead to a sudden drop of 14% of all visits, corresponding to a loss of EUR 350 million per year and the potential loss of 2 000 local jobs. Similarly, it has been shown that people living in the surroundings of water bodies benefit from increased property values when wastewater treatment measures ensure a certain quality of water bodies (OECD, 2011[12]) (OECD, 2018[13]).

Some countries have assessed economy-wide benefits of water quality improvements. For instance, the **United States** Environmental Protection Agency estimates the net benefits of water pollution legislation in the last 30 years at about USD 11 billion annually, or about USD 109 per household. In the **United Kingdom**, several studies estimating benefits and costs of measures to implement the EU Water Framework Directive have been showing a net benefit in England and Wales of USD 10 million. In the **Netherlands**, similar cost-benefit analyses showed that monetised benefits were significantly less than estimated costs, but an important range of benefits could not be monetised. Assessments would greatly benefit from a more thorough and systematic valuation of direct and indirect benefits of treated wastewater (OECD, 2011[12]).

Switzerland was the first country to roll out a national strategy to assess investments that reduce pharmaceutical residues in water, essentially by upgrading treatment levels in wastewater treatment plants. The Waters Protection Act was revised in 2014 and it mandates the upgrade of 100 wastewater treatment plants to remove selected residues. The total investment cost to upgrade the 100 wastewater treatment plants was estimated to be around USD 1 billion, plus an additional USD 115 million per year for operation and maintenance costs. The majority of the capital costs (75%) have been covered by the national budget. The remaining investment, operation and maintenance costs are covered by municipalities as well as a new (2016) federal sewage tax of EUR 9/person/year (OECD, 2019[2]). The **Netherlands** pioneer a life-cycle approach, which combines initiatives from a range of stakeholders all along the value chain, from drug development to manufacturing and use and waste management (see Box 4.5).

4.2. Risk mitigation

The Recommendation highlights the need to "identify, assess and endeavour to mitigate risks associated with investments that negatively affect the natural integrity of rivers, lakes, aquifers and wetlands, their hydro morphological conditions, the natural water retention capacity of the basins or ecosystem functioning".

Strengthening valuations of water pollution in Environmental Impact Assessments (EIAs), which are required for infrastructure development projects in most Adherent countries, can help to identify, assess and mitigate any risks arising from these investments and identify trade-offs and co-benefits. EIAs are usually reviewed by locally relevant committee of public officials, experts and residents' representatives, such as in **Korea**. The **European Union** has published guidance with practical steps to be followed in a EIAs (OECD, 2018[8]).

4.3. Reduction of water pollution

The Recommendation encourages Adherents to "take measures to reduce, to the extent necessary, the pollution of all waters and in particular the pollution of surface waters resulting in eutrophication, with particular reference to the problem arising from the transfer of nutrient-loaded waters across frontiers or to the sea. These measures should ensure compliance with the water quality objectives and targets mentioned above".

In **Europe**, nutrient pollution, leading to eutrophication, is a widespread problem which occurs in about 30% of water bodies in 17 member states. **Denmark** uses cost-effectiveness analysis to manage risk of eutrophication (OECD, 2018[14]). In **Canada**, federal programmes implemented at provincial level such as the Environmental Farm Plans and the Environmental Stewardship Incentive aim to reduce eutrophication and algal blooms, for instance by requiring buffer strips around surface water bodies and groundwater sources (OECD, 2017[7]).

Regulating surface water quality in transboundary basins requires, at a minimum, that the riparian states agree on joint criteria for the assessment of surface water quality. Joint criteria help to assure that countries make compatible assessments and draw conclusions about water quality. Building on such criteria, the **United States** and **Canada** have established joint surface quality targets to be achieved on both sides of the border as well as have coordinated their water management measures. This can be a good example for Adherents (Box 4.4).

Box 4.4. Joint management of water quality in North America's Great Lakes

The Lake Erie, bordering the States of New York, Pennsylvania, Ohio and Michigan, and the Canadian province of Ontario, has been a subject of concern due to nutrient overloading from fertilisers, and human and animal waste, leading to eutrophication, hypoxia and algal blooms.

The 1972 Great Lakes Water Quality Agreement helped improved the situation with reduced phosphorus from point sources. However, diffuse sources from agriculture and domestic lawns have remained largely unaccounted for, and since the mid-1990s, Lake Erie has been returning to a more eutrophic state. For instance, in 2014, the eutrophication of Lake Erie resulted in a seven-day tap water ban for Toledo, Ohio when blooms of toxic algae shut down drinking water supplies from the lake, affecting more than 400 000 people. Furthermore, the water ban occurred after the city of Toledo increased spending on water treatment chemicals - USD 4 million in 2013.

In acknowledgement of the ongoing water quality problems, the hypoxia-based loading targets were revised in the 2012 Great Lakes Water Quality Agreement, and in 2016 the governments of Canada and the United States announced bi-national phosphorus load reduction targets of 40% for Lake Erie.

Source: (OECD, 2017[7]) using Scavia et al., 2014

4.4. Cost-effectiveness

The Recommendation encourages Adherents to "foster the most cost-effective measures for improving water quality, whilst keeping polluters and users accountable as much as possible through:

- A targeted action on pollutants of particular significance at the appropriate scale (catchment, basin, or aquifer), on the basis of such characteristics as toxicity, persistence, bio-accumulation, and risk to human and environmental health.
- The application of pollution control measures as close to the source as possible taking into consideration alternative cost-effective options in case of disproportionate costs.
- Integrated pollution control so that water pollution control measures do not lead to uncontrolled pollution transfers to other water resources or to soil or air systems."

In light of the Polluter Pays and the Beneficiary Pays Principles, countries are holding polluters accountable for the water pollution they may cause. Countries are using pollution charges, taxes on inputs (such as fertilisers and pesticides) and sewer user charges to send appropriate signal and to generate revenues to address pollution (see chapters 7 and 8 for more information on the state of play). The application of the Polluter Pays Principle is less costly and more commonly applied for the control of point source pollution than diffuse sources (OECD, 2017[15]). It can be applied at different stages of the pollution chain (Box 4.5).

The **European Union** is one rare jurisdiction that applies the Polluter Pays principle in the agriculture sector. The Nitrates Directive (1991) aims to protect water quality by preventing nitrates from agricultural sources reaching ground and surface waters. This Directive requires member states to identify Nitrate Vulnerable Zones (NVZs),[4] to develop codes of good practices for all farmers and implement action programmes for NVZs. These actions include the mandatory application of the codes and of other measures to limit the quantity of nitrogen applied with animal manures. Later embedded into the requirements under the Water Framework Directive, the Nitrates Directive took a long time to be implemented by member states, with results starting to be visible for surface water, but less obvious for groundwater. Some member states were found in violation of their obligation under this directive (Gruère, Ashley and Cadilhon, 2018[16]).

Box 4.5. Identified measures to reduce pharmaceutical residues at different stages of the pharmaceutical chain in the Netherlands

The **Netherlands** has identified 17 possible measures to reduce human pharmaceutical residues at different stages of the pharmaceutical chain. Depending on the measures, the sectors responsible include the government, water authorities, pharmaceutical companies, research institutions or Municipalities and chemists.

Examples of measure include:

- **Environmental monitoring**: Identify pharmaceuticals that have negative environmental effects, Identify effects of veterinary pharmaceuticals in water, Quantify emissions of veterinary pharmaceuticals to surface water and groundwater.
- **Development and authorisation**: Develop 'green medicines' that have less environmental impact, Develop management system for environmental risks of medicines (Eco Pharmaco Stewardship), Improve access to environmental data on APIs
- **Prescription and consumption**: Identify pairs of pharmaceuticals with same medic effect, but different environmental impact, Research prevention and adequate use of pharmaceuticals, Identify possible measures in the phase of 'prescription and use'
- **Waste and wastewater treatment:** Establish collection schemes of surplus pharmaceuticals, Evaluate improved treatment at WWTPs, including overview of existing innovative treatment options and overview of costs, Identify WWTPs with highest impact on aquatic ecology and drinking water sources, Start pilots with improved treatment at existing WWTPs Waste & wastewater.
- **Cross-cutting**: Develop communication instrument to explain the pharmaceutical chain, Develop communication strategy and execute, Learn from best practices abroad, Put issue on international agenda (e.g. river basin commissions of Rhine and Meuse, European Commission, others)

Source: (OECD, 2019[2])

Some tools and mechanisms are helping Adherents overcome challenges related to the identification and targeting of polluters. For instance, the **EU**, **United States**, **Australia** and **New Zealand** manage pollution with computer modelling in catchments (Box 4.5) (OECD, 2018[8]). **Korea** uses collective accountability at the catchment level, as total pollution load is monitored at that scale, and farmers active in the catchment are collectively accountable (OECD, 2017[17]). Many Adherents are using proxies such as taxes on inputs (e.g. fertilisers, pesticides, cleaning products) or land use (e.g. paved urban surfaces, livestock numbers, intensive land use) (chapter 8). However these taxes are not always effective due to the low response they induce, except at very high levels (Sud, 2020[10]). In **Norway**, the pesticides tax, revised in 1999 to better reflect environmental and health risks, successfully encouraged the use of less toxic pesticide. While it resulted only in a slight decline in overall quantity of pesticide sold, the pesticide tax induced a shift towards using pesticides with lower environmental and health risks (Ibid.).

While it can be difficult to estimate reliably pollution costs, Adherents are using new data sources for monitoring and justifying action (see Box 4.5 above). They are also using market-based mechanisms to reveal pollution costs. The point-diffuse source water quality trading to reduce nutrient pollution of Chesapeake Bay in the **United States** and the Lake Taupō market to cap nitrogen emissions at the catchment scale in **New Zealand**, the world's first diffuse source pollution-related market in the world, are illustrative (OECD, 2017[7]).

The Recommendation also invites Adherents to "consider the most cost-effective measures to tackle water quality issues, whilst applying the Polluter Pays Principle as much as possible where it is mentioned in the legal and regulatory framework, and promoting it where absent".

In line with the Polluter Pays principle under the EU Water Framework Directive, the association of German Water Suppliers presented a proposal for setting up an extended producer responsibility (EPR) scheme to require certain pharmaceutical manufacturing companies to contribute to the recovering costs of advanced wastewater treatment plant upgrades. While the tool comes with some practical issues (OECD, 2020[19]) it is an interesting development, well-aligned with the requirements of the Recommendation.

4.5. Cost-effectiveness and Polluter Pays Principle

The Recommendation encourages Adherents to "combine regulatory, voluntary and economic instruments to provide continuing incentives for polluters to reduce and control pollution of water resources".

Most Adherents have a range of policy instruments to promote water quality and tackle pollution. This chapter provides an inventory of the most common ones and illustrates some combinations.

Adherents use regulatory instruments to limit the discharge of pollutants into water bodies. **New Zealand** has regulated point-source pollution effectively through discharge permits for limiting industrial and urban wastewater discharge in its 1991 Resource Management Act (OECD, 2017[11]). New Zealand also requires regional governments to manage point and diffuse discharges within set environmental limits, which are already showing their impact with some water bodies making significant recoveries, such as the Rotorua Lakes. Tighter regulations on industrial wastewater have resulted in a significant reduction in heavy metals in **Japan** (OECD, 2017[7]). In cases where standards are not sufficient, or as a precaution, some countries can proceed to ban an activity, as illustrated by the worldwide ban of DDT, or the annual two-month fishing ban in the Pearl River system in **China** to restore fish numbers and improve water quality (OECD, 2012[20]). Finally, **Costa Rica** set effluent limit values for polluting parameters such as biochemical oxygen demand (BOD), chemical oxygen demand (COD), phosphorus, nitrates, acidity (pH), fats and oils and suspended solids in its 2007 Law on the Discharge and Reuse of Wastewater. Additional limits are set for a group of hazardous substances (OECD, 2012[21]).

Voluntary agreements or commitments to take actions to improve the water environment are commonly used across Adherent countries. They are unilateral commitments taken by firms or cities. There are also negotiated agreements such the **United Kingdom**'s Pesticides Voluntary Initiative which promotes responsible pesticide use (OECD, 2012[20]). **New Zealand**'s "Sustainable Dairying: Water Accord" is a success story to manage water pollution related to dairy farming. Adherents are also using payments for eco-system services to improve water-related environment such as the Tasmanian Forest Conservation Fund programme in **Australia** or Vittel's (Nestle Water) scheme in **France** (OECD, 2012[20]).

Economic instruments are used by many Adherents to incentivise pollution reduction and fund water quality-related upgrades. Most Adherents are taxing environmentally harmful products, and apply pollution charges on emissions. For example, a number of countries are using effluent discharge taxes (Figure 4.2) (further details are provided in chapter 8). They also provide incentives such as subsidies to upgrade infrastructure. Several Adherents have also established tradable permits to reduce pollution and negative externalities, such as in the **United States** and in **New Zealand** (OECD, 2017[7]). **France** provides financial incentives (EUR 10 million) for stimulating new innovative projects to manage contaminants of emerging concerns and empowering local stakeholders. The selected projects target domestic, industrial, diffuse and multiple sources of pollution and include solutions for better diagnostics, cost-efficient reduction of CECs and changes in practices of various types of stakeholders (OECD, 2019[2]).

Figure 4.2. Countries with effluent discharge tax

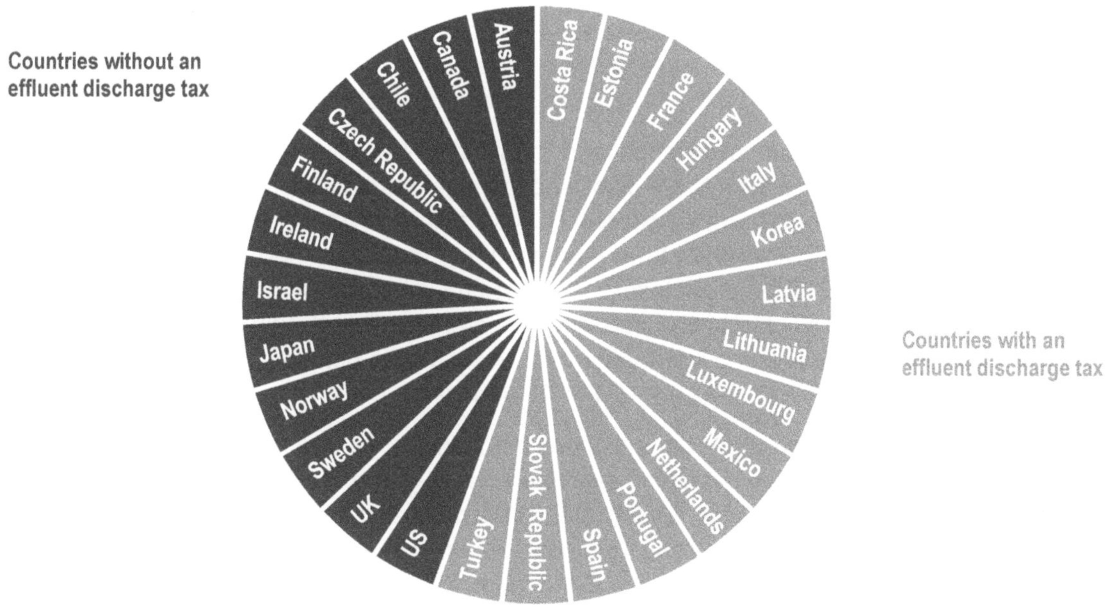

Note: Responses to the question: "Does your country have an effluent discharge tax?".
Source: 2019 survey on the implementation of the OECD Council Recommendation on Water; 27 responses received, including 26 Adherents.

Policies to promote the collection and treatment of (domestic and industrial) wastewater typically combine regulation (standards on required levels of treatment before a wastewater can be returned to the environment), information (on water quality and the performance of utilities and service provided) and market mechanisms (a charge on pollution load, that makes pollution costly and possibly generates revenues to invest in abatement). Such a combination is exemplified in the UWWTD, part of the **European Commission**'s acquis on water.

In the case of agriculture, twenty two Adherents use a combination of regulatory, economic and (voluntary) information instruments. Regulatory instruments are the most common, followed by economic and information instruments. For instance, **Canada** has a Federal Act on water quality and provinces apply their own water quality regulations. Via the Canadian Agricultural Partnership, the federal government supports cost-share programmes to increase the adoption of farm best management practices to reduce pollution. Agriculture and Agri-Food Canada has also launched a new initiative that will facilitate communication and knowledge transfer between researchers and producers about sustainable farming practice. **Denmark** combines carrot and sticks by implementing a targeted regulation aiming to reduce nutrient pollution at the source, beyond Nitrates Directive requirements, payments via the rural development program to incentivise producers to do better than regulatory minimum, and collaboration with farmers' organisation to facilitate collective measures.[5]

4.6. Compliance

The Council also recommends to "set up mechanisms to monitor and enforce compliance with regulatory provisions. Enforcement should be targeted, making use of all available data sources. It should build on clear, transparent and proportionate enforcement rules, procedures, penalties, incentives and tools to achieve regulatory objectives cost-effectively".

Although Adherents are setting water quality objectives and policies, there is evidence of implementation gaps due to insufficient compliance. Facility-specific permits translate environmental policies into enforceable conditions. In the **United Kingdom** although the permitting framework only covers around 2% of registered businesses, all businesses are covered by general legal requirements, for example, to fulfil their "duty of care" with respect to water pollution prevention (OECD, 2009[22]). Countries monitor compliance with regulatory effluent limits and impose fines in case of breach of requirements.

Compliance is promoted through assistance and information-based tools about firms' environmental behaviour and performance. These tools are also used to trigger market reactions and community pressure against violators. For instance, the **United States** Toxics Release Inventory (TRI) provides information to the public on releases of toxic chemicals from manufacturing facilities. The European Pollutant Release and Transfer Register (E-PRTR) is a disclosure tool that provides data on amounts of pollutant releases to air, water and land as well as off-site transfers of waste and of pollutants in waste water, from over more than 30 000 industrial facilities. Some information on releases from diffuse sources is also available and will be gradually enhanced (OECD, 2009[22]) (E-PRTR website).

Compliance is monitored through inspections, various monitoring tools and with self monitoring processes. In **EU** countries with fully integrated permitting systems such as in **France** and **Finland**, all the inspections are multimedia (e.g. covering air, water, wastewater, hazardous and solid waste). In the United Kingdom and the Netherlands, where the permitting regimes remain differentiated, both integrated and water-specific inspections are used. Finland relies more and more on self-monitoring and reporting of wastewater discharges (OECD, 2009[22]).

In cases of non-compliance with water quality regulations, countries often apply fines and more stringent control to enforce regulations, according to the 2019 OECD Implementation Survey (Figure 4.3). Faced with continued non-compliance of nutrient pollution regulations, several Adherents have adopted innovative approaches. The Scottish Environment Protection Agency in the United Kingdom decided to re-shift its activities from notification of non-compliance to developing solutions directly with farmers to achieve compliance, achieving some visible progress. Ireland's regulators have used behavioural sciences to improve their messaging with farmers, using more personalised communication and engaging into farm advice where needed (Gruère and Le Boëdec, 2019[10]).

Figure 4.3. Types of penalties used in case of non-compliance with water quality regulation

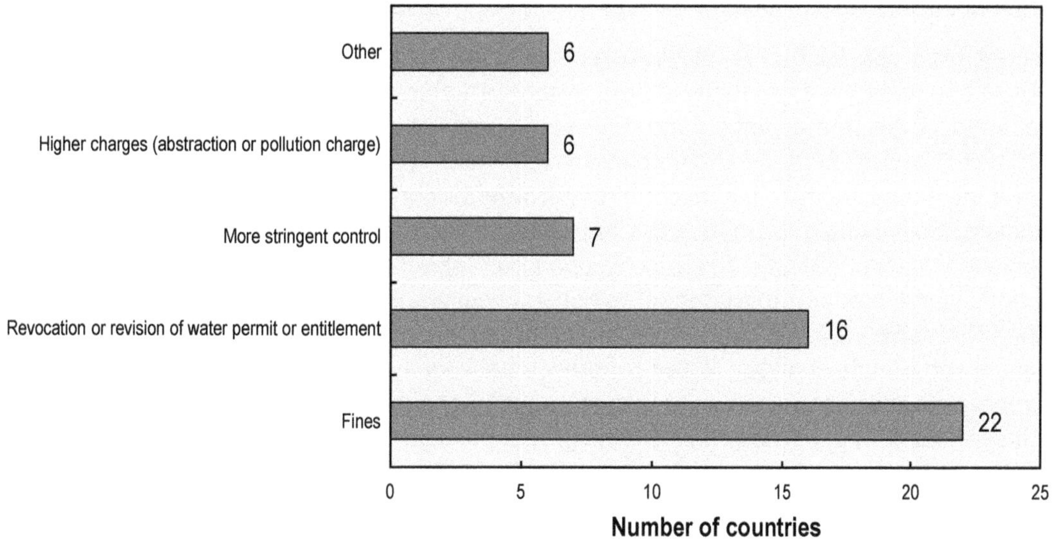

Note: Responses to the question: "What kind of penalties are used in case of non-compliance with water quality regulations?." Multiple responses were possible.
Source: 2019 survey on the implementation of the OECD Council Recommendation on Water; 27 responses received, including 26 Adherents.

Finally, a competent authority can also force an offender to carry out the clean-up and then administratively recover the costs incurred from the responsible party such as in the **United States** where this can be done only through a federal court. The Environment Agency of England and Wales (**United Kingdom**) can invoice the polluter directly for cleaning up a toxic spill in water. The responsibility for enforcing remediation or undertaking it and recover the costs from the operator is the subject of the 2004 **EU** Environmental Liability Directive (OECD, 2009[22]).

4.7. Sustainable use of water-related ecosystems

The Council encourages Adherents "to take measures to protect, restore and promote sustainable use of water-related ecosystems, halt and reverse degradation, and halt biodiversity loss".

Indeed, improving water quality is valuable for environmental uses such as the provision of fish habitat and ecosystem health (OECD, 2017[7]). Scaling up nature-based solutions has been a way for many Adherents to improve water-related ecosystems (see chapter 5 for more details).

4.8. Coherence between water and sectoral policies

The Council also encourages Adherents "to take the following measures to address sector-specific issues".

Adherents are encouraged "to foster coherence between water and sectoral policies, e.g. industry, energy, nature, drinking water, health care and agriculture. For the latter, identify and reduce to the greatest extent possible any harmful incentives and practices that have adverse environmental or water-harmful effects (e.g. subsidies for fertiliser and pesticides that are harmful to water)."

The strong interlinkages between water and other policies (such as agriculture, forestry, industry, mining, energy, environment, drinking water, solid waste, health, fisheries, urban development, spatial planning and land use, tourism and recreation) require robust mainstreaming of water into the policies and plans of sectors that affect water availability and use. Policy coherence can help overcome possible tensions among different sectors responsible for taking and financing action.

More coherent policy approaches are slowly beginning to take shape as seen in the case of the agricultural sector. OECD countries have gradually shifted away from output and input support and most distorting agricultural support, which may encourage the use of water or impact nutrient pollution (Gruère and Le Boëdec, 2019[10]; DeBoe, 2020[23]; Henderson and Lankoski, 2019[24]) to decoupled payments and to a limited extent payments that take into account environmental concerns and help to reduce water pollution from agriculture. Still, much more efforts are needed with 50% of support in OECD countries potentially environmentally impactful (OECD, 2019[25]). Support can take the form of nitrogen fertiliser subsidies to stimulate agricultural production. Nitrogen, which moves among environmental media and takes on multiple forms, creates multiple risks to the environment (e.g. to air quality, to water quality through eutrophication, and climate change). Policy coherence between nitrogen pollution management policy and other environmental and sectoral needs thus to be sought. For example, depending on the types of fertiliser and soil, nitrogen fertiliser subsidies can increase greenhouse gas emissions of crops. **China**, for instance, has taken steps to phase out fertiliser subsidies (OECD, 2018[14]).

More generally, despite progress since 2009, agriculture and water policies remain insufficiently aligned (Figure 4.4). Results from the OECD Survey on water and agriculture policy changes were used to derive relative alignment indices for each country and section of the Recommendation (Gruère, Shigemitsu and Crawford, 2020[9]).[6] The average alignment score of Adherents policies with the OECD's water quality recommendations is 0.54, or close to half of its potential maximum value. The maximum alignment score in 2019 is much below that of other recommendations, indicating that more efforts are needed by all Adherents.

Figure 4.4. Alignment of agriculture and water policies with section 4 recommendations on water quality

Changes from 2009 to 2019, Scores range from 0 to 1. Higher scores indicate a higher alignment

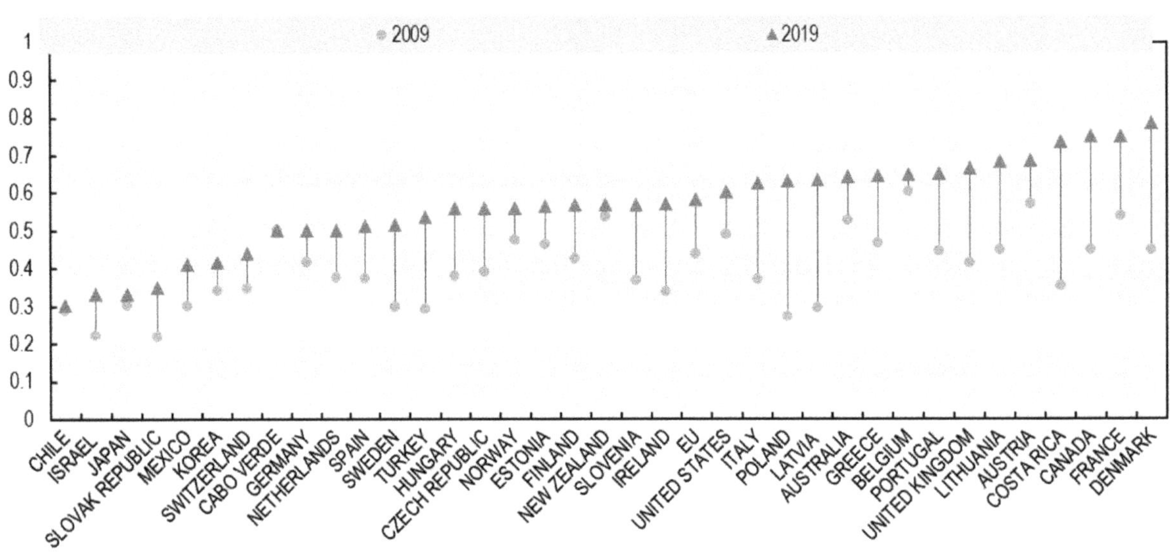

Note: Colombia and Iceland did not provide responses.
Source: (Gruère, Shigemitsu and Crawford, 2020[9])

The Recommendation encourages Adherents "to adopt the appropriate financial, managerial and technical measures to ensure that wastewater treatment systems: are built and operated in a cost-efficient manner; take into consideration the topography and future population trends; contribute to water quality objectives; and allow for resource recovery, energy and water efficiency and reuse to conserve water."

Substantial investments in wastewater treatment plants and progress in controlling point sources of pollution have contributed to significant improvements in water quality in recent decades (OECD, 2017[7]). In more than one third of OECD countries over 80% of the population are connected to a sewage treatment plant with at least secondary treatment (OECD, 2020[26]).

Recent work by Eureau (the union of private water utilities in Europe) indicates that very little is known on the state of the asset and the rate of renewal of existing wastewater collection and treatment systems (OECD, 2020[19]). On-going discussions in Europe on the comparative strengths and limitations of Individual and other appropriate sanitation Systems (IAS) illustrate complexities related to the design of appropriate infrastructures that reflect local conditions (geography and topography, density of settlements, sensitivity of receiving environments, etc.) (OECD, 2020[19]).

The Recommendation encourages Adherents "to pay particular attention to achieving sustainable management and conservation of fishing resources and other aquatic life in freshwater and related coastal areas at the local, national and international levels, and ensure co-ordination of all relevant authorities, to the extent possible".

A number of coastal countries target much of their efforts to reduce pollution that contributes to eutrophic zones in coastal areas. For instance, **Lithuania**'s Water Development Program for 2017-2023 sets the goal of reducing eutrophication-promoting nutrients entering the Curonian Lagoon and the Baltic Sea, by reducing inflows of nitrogen and phosphorus compounds (with specific quantitative targets). In **Canada**, the Federal Government has also committed CAD 44.84 million over five years (2017-2022) to Canada's Great Lakes Protection Initiative, CAD 26 million of which is allocated to prevent toxic and nuisance algae in Lake Erie. This includes development of watershed plans to identify priority areas for phosphorus management and implementation of phosphorus reduction measures outlined in the 2018 Canada-Ontario Lake Erie Action Plan.[7]

In **Norway**, support is provided for assisting practices that benefit wetlands and ecosystems in farmed landscapes, and for establishing ponds and constructed wetlands. In the **United States**, the US Department of Agriculture's Wildlife Habitat Incentives Program provides financial and technical assistance for improvement of fish and wildlife habitat. In addition, recent US Farm Bills have included swampbuster provisions to discourage the conversion of wetlands or highly erodible lands to crop production through the loss of eligibility for federal program benefits.[8]

References

DeBoe, G. (2020), "Impacts of agricultural policies on productivity and sustainability performance in agriculture: A literature review", *OECD Food, Agriculture and Fisheries Papers*, No. 141, OECD Publishing, Paris, https://dx.doi.org/10.1787/6bc916e7-en. [23]

Gruère, G., C. Ashley and J. Cadilhon (2018), "Reforming water policies in agriculture: Lessons from past reforms", *OECD Food, Agriculture and Fisheries Papers*, No. 113, OECD Publishing, Paris, https://dx.doi.org/10.1787/1826beee-en. [16]

Gruère, G. and H. Le Boëdec (2019), "Navigating pathways to reform water policies in agriculture", *OECD Food, Agriculture and Fisheries Papers*, No. 128, OECD Publishing, Paris, https://dx.doi.org/10.1787/906cea2b-en. [10]

Gruère, G., M. Shigemitsu and S. Crawford (2020), "Agriculture and water policy changes: Stocktaking and alignment with OECD and G20 recommendations", *OECD Food, Agriculture and Fisheries Papers*, No. 144, OECD Publishing, Paris, https://dx.doi.org/10.1787/f35e64af-en. [9]

Henderson, B. and J. Lankoski (2019), *The environmental impacts of agriculture policies*, OECD Food, Agriculture, and Fisheries Papers No. 130, OECD Publishing, Paris, https://doi.org/10.1787/add0f27c-en. [24]

OECD (2020), *Environment at a Glance Indicators*, OECD Publishing, Paris, https://dx.doi.org/10.1787/ac4b8b89-en. [26]

OECD (2020), *Financing Water Supply, Sanitation and Flood Protection: Challenges in EU Member States and Policy Options*, OECD Studies on Water, OECD Publishing, Paris, https://dx.doi.org/10.1787/6893cdac-en. [19]

OECD (2019), *OECD Environmental Performance Reviews: Australia 2019*, OECD Publishing, http://dx.doi.org/10.1787/9789264310452-en. [4]

OECD (2019), *Agricultural Policy Monitoring and Evaluation 2019*, OECD Publishing, Paris, http://dx.doi.org/10.1787/39bfe6f3-en. [25]

OECD (2019), *Pharmaceutical Residues in Freshwater: Hazards and Policy Responses*, OECD Studies on Water, OECD Publishing, Paris, https://dx.doi.org/10.1787/c936f42d-en. [2]

OECD (2018), *Cost-Benefit Analysis and the Environment: Further Developments and Policy Use*, https://doi.org/10.1787/9789264085169-en. [13]

OECD (2018), *Human Acceleration of the Nitrogen Cycle: Managing Risks and Uncertainty*, OECD Publishing, Paris, https://dx.doi.org/10.1787/9789264307438-en. [14]

OECD (2018), *Managing the Water-Energy-Land-Food Nexus in Korea: Policies and Governance Options*, OECD Studies on Water, OECD Publishing, Paris, https://dx.doi.org/10.1787/9789264306523-en. [8]

OECD (2017), *Accession review of Lithuania in the field of environment*, http://dx.doi.org/ENV/EPOC/ACS(2017)1. [1]

OECD (2017), *Diffuse Pollution, Degraded Waters: Emerging Policy Solutions*, OECD Studies on Water, OECD Publishing, Paris, https://dx.doi.org/10.1787/9789264269064-en. [7]

OECD (2017), *Diffuse Pollution, Degraded Waters: Emerging Policy Solutions*, OECD Studies on Water, OECD Publishing, Paris, https://dx.doi.org/10.1787/9789264269064-en. [15]

OECD (2017), *Enhancing Water Use Efficiency in Korea: Policy Issues and Recommendations*, OECD Studies on Water, OECD Publishing, Paris, https://dx.doi.org/10.1787/9789264281707-en. [17]

OECD (2017), *OECD Environmental Performance Reviews: New Zealand 2017*, OECD Environmental Performance Reviews, OECD Publishing, Paris, https://dx.doi.org/10.1787/9789264268203-en. [11]

OECD (2015), *Water and Cities: Ensuring Sustainable Futures*, OECD Studies on Water, OECD Publishing, Paris, https://dx.doi.org/10.1787/9789264230149-en. [5]

OECD (2013), *OECD Environmental Performance Reviews: Italy 2013*, OECD Environmental Performance Reviews, OECD Publishing, Paris, https://dx.doi.org/10.1787/9789264186378-en. [6]

OECD (2012), *OECD Environmental Outlook to 2050: The Consequences of Inaction*, OECD Publishing, Paris, https://dx.doi.org/10.1787/9789264122246-en. [20]

OECD (2012), *OECD Environmental Outlook to 2050: The Consequences of Inaction*, OECD Publishing, Paris, https://dx.doi.org/10.1787/9789264122246-en. [21]

OECD (2011), *Benefits of Investing in Water and Sanitation: An OECD Perspective*, OECD Studies on Water, OECD Publishing, https://doi.org/10.1787/9789264100817-en. [12]

OECD (2009), *Ensuring Environmental Compliance: Trends and Good Practices*, OECD Publishing, Paris, https://dx.doi.org/10.1787/9789264059597-en. [22]

OECD, FAO, IIASA (2020), *Towards a G20 Action Plan on Water. Background note to the G20 Saudi Presidency*. [3]

Sud, M. (2020), *Managing the Biodiversity Impacts of Fertiliser and Pesticide Use: Overview and insights from trends and policies across selected OECD countries*, No. 155s, OECD Publishing, Paris, http://www.oecd.org/officialdocuments/publicdisplaydocumentpdf/?cote=ENV/WKP(2020)2&docLanguage=En. [18]

Notes

[1] 2019 OECD Survey on water and agriculture policy changes.

[2] Examples include pharmaceuticals, industrial and household chemicals, personal care products, pesticides, manufactured nanomaterials, and their transformation products.

[3] 2019 OECD Survey on water and agriculture policy changes.

[4] NVZs are defined as zones where nitrates concentration exceed 50mg/Lor that are subject to eutrophication.

[5] 2019 OECD Survey on water and agriculture policy changes.

[6] The used methods and its limitations are discussed in detail in OECD (2020[9]).

[7] 2019 OECD Survey on water and agriculture policy changes.

[8] Ibid.

5. Managing water risks and disasters

This chapter presents Adherents' experience with the management of water risks and disasters, in line with the OECD Recommendation on Water. The chapter explores how Adherents manage water risks and disasters in a cooperative way. It highlights examples of risk assessment and awareness raising efforts carried out by Adherents, as well as setting and revising acceptable levels of water risks. It also explores prevention and mitigation, and emergency responses measures. It includes investment in social policies and financial mechanisms to minimise disruption, while ensuring transparency, accountability and public awareness in decision-making. It describes progress in policy coherence across sectors. Finally, the chapter focuses on water risks related to climate change in agriculture and cities.

Every year, water-related disasters such as tropical storms, floods and droughts account for the majority of disasters that take lives, destroy property and cripple livelihoods (Figure 5.1). The number of people at risk from water-related disasters is projected to increase from 1.2 billion to 1.6 billion over the next 30 years (OECD, 2019[1]). This will represent around 20% of the world population. While the majority of these people live in developing economies, the value of economic assets at risk is concentrated in OECD members.

Figure 5.1. Number of water-related and non-water-related disasters in OECD countries

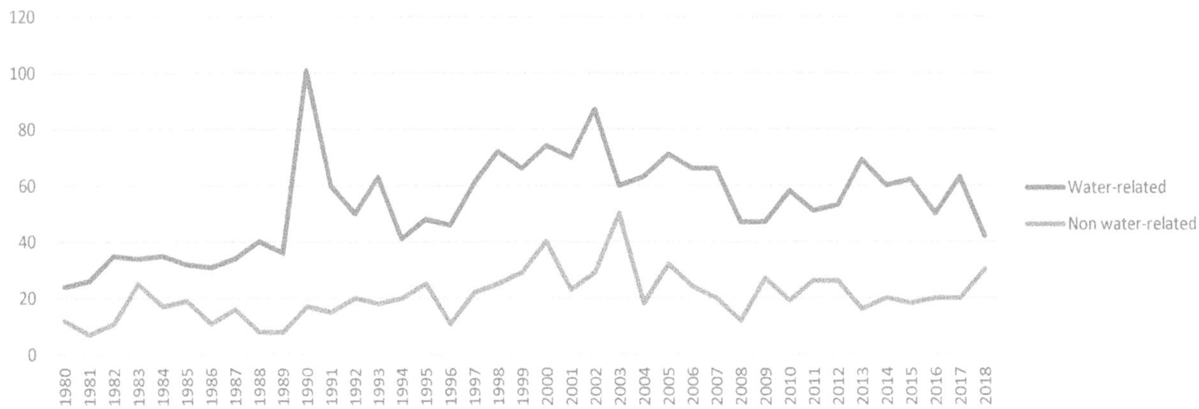

Source: EM-DAT; The OFDA/CRED International Disaster Database, - Université catholique de Louvain (UCL) - CRED, D. Guha-Sapir - www.emdat.be, Brussels, Belgium.

The Recommendation calls on Adherents to "manage water risks and disasters in a co-operative way, adopt and review a water risk management policy as an all-hazards approach to country risk governance" (OECD, 2016[2]). Adherents have made steady progress in preparing for water-related disasters by investing in risk assessments, risk awareness, prevention and mitigation measures, and emergency response capabilities. For Adherents that are members of the **European Union**, many of these actions were already given priority pursuant to national implementation of the European Floods Directive, which has been effective since 2007. Other Adherents have established national risk management frameworks that respond to and that take into account of all aspects of water risk management. An overview of recent trends in water related disasters substantiates the need for Adherents to sustain, and in some cases increase, these efforts.

5.1. Managing water risks and disasters in a cooperative way

Cooperation in managing water-related risks and disasters is essential as river basins frequently transcend national borders. The risks and challenges associated with river basin flood management are increasingly shared amongst neighbouring countries. The 2019 OECD Implementation Survey indicates that a vast majority of responding Adherents share monitoring data and information on water levels, flow rates and water quality as means to map and forecast transboundary risks. A smaller number share water management plans or develop joint emergency water management procedures and exercises. Some Adherents even have experience with co-financing structural disaster risk reduction measures. Other forms of cooperation include bilateral conventions and exchange platforms in place for maritime pollution emergencies.

Experience, in particular in Europe, illustrates good practices in cooperation for the management of water-related risks and disasters. The Convention on the Protection of the Rhine establishes international cooperation between France, Germany, Luxembourg, Netherlands, Switzerland and the European Union, including on joint flood prevention and protection measures. Parties to the Convention typically share information on actions taken in their territory to protect the Rhine. In the event of incidents or accidents that might threaten water quality or in the event of imminent flooding, parties inform the Commission and the Contracting Parties likely to be affected in accordance with the warning alert plans.

The United States and Canada have adopted numerous agreements dealing with water management. The Columbia River Treaty, for example, required Canada to build three hydroelectric dams. In return, Canada received 50% of the electricity generation and payment for increased flood control benefits from the United States. Similarly, water is one of the defining issues in the relationship between the US and Mexico as the two countries share three catchments – the Rio Grande, Colorado River and the Tijuana River. While much of the focus of the cooperation has been on allocating water resources, infrastructure construction and water quality, a trend towards a more holistic and integrated approach to water management has emerged more recently, particularly with respect to the environmental health of the river basins.

The overall challenge that impedes cooperation consists in the numerous jurisdictional layers and a variety of policies on water-related risks. Nonetheless, advancing synergies arising from cooperation offers unique opportunities to enhance the efficiency and effectives of plans and programmes.

5.2. Risk assessment

Given the inherent uncertainty in the location, timing, severity and impacts of water related hazards, Adherents to the Recommendation should invest in "risk assessment to help prioritise disaster risk reduction, emergency management capabilities and the design of financial protection strategies (which are used to manage the financial impact of disasters, ensure adequate capacity to manage and mitigate the costs of disaster risk, thereby reducing the financial burden and economic costs of disasters and enabling rapid recovery in economic activity). Depending on issues at stake risk assessment could take account of private responses (adaptation) to risk and reactions to disasters (response)".

Adherents use risk assessments to provide a scientific basis for a wide range of public decisions including: where to develop new communities or expand existing ones; prioritising what communities to protect in a floodplain and which communities to relocate; identifying individual properties to notify about exposure and targeting programmes to increase their resistance and resilience; supporting development of flood detection, forecasting and warning systems; designing emergency response and recovery plans; and calculating potential damages to design insurance programmes that spread risk and accelerate recovery (OECD, 2018[3]).

The majority of responding Adherents have taken multiple steps to improve the accuracy, comparability and utility of sub-national water-related risk assessments. Figure 5.2 shows that 85% of respondents developed guidance and standards to assess water-related risks. It also indicates 78% have undertaken spatial mapping of water-related risks. In **Switzerland**, the federal law obliges cantons and communities to establish hazard maps for a range of natural perils, including floods (OECD, 2018[3]). Adherents use spatial mapping for many purposes, for example to identify water related infrastructure and public services exposed to flood risks. In the **United Kingdom** over 55% of water and sewage pumping stations/treatment works are in flood risk areas, with 34% at significant risk. Among the identified good practices for Adherents to learn from, **Portugal** has completed a flood risk and vulnerability mapping exercise that considers the potential impact of various climate change scenarios.

Figure 5.2. Actions taken to assess water-related risks

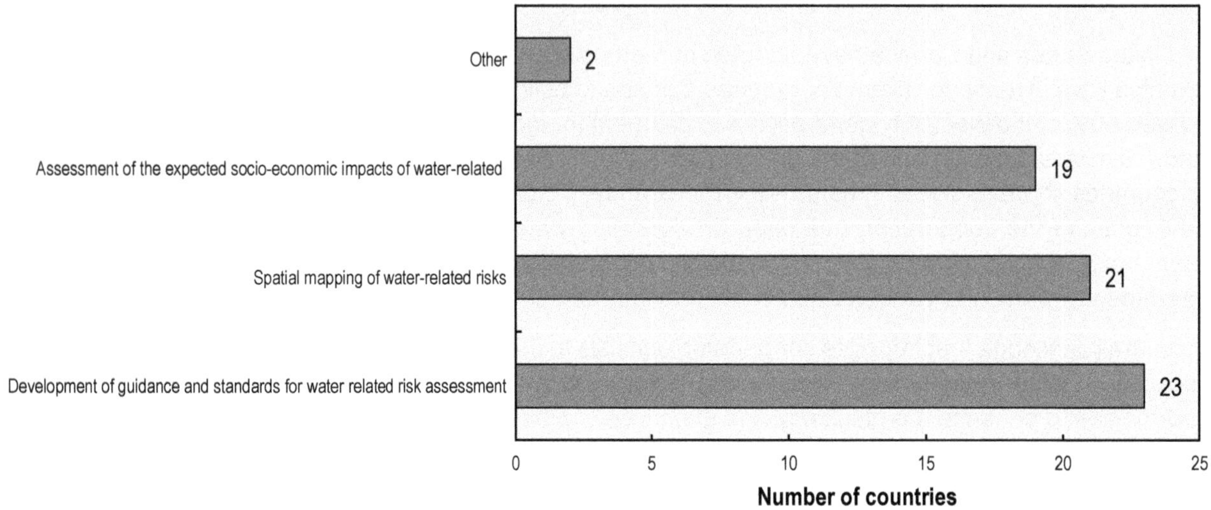

Note: Responses to question: "To assess water-related risks, which of the following tasks have been undertaken?". Multiple responses were possible.
Source: 2019 survey on the implementation of the OECD Council Recommendation on Water; 27 responses received, including 26 Adherents.

Indeed flood risk is likely to increase among many Adherents due to climate change and continued development in hazard prone areas. 70% of respondents have assessed socio-economic impacts of water related risks. In England the expected annual damages to residential and non-residential properties at risk from flooding from rivers and the sea, including hospitals and schools, is over USD 1.2 billion. Already in the **United Kingdom** the national flood risk assessment shows there are 2.4 million properties at risk from flooding from rivers and the sea in England, with more exposed to surface water than other forms of flooding (UK Environment Agency, 2009[4]).

Figure 5.3 indicates a higher number of respondents conduct risk assessments at basin and local levels for river floods and water pollution. This reflects the relatively high frequency of river floods compared to coastal floods, and daily public health risks that polluted drinking water poses. The economic and environmental impacts of coastal floods, however, should not be overlooked. Coastal concentrations of populations, trade infrastructure, tourism and petro-chemical industries underscore the need for coastal risk assessments. Surprisingly, some Adherents with coastlines report that they do not conduct coastal flood risk assessments.

Figure 5.3. Coverage of risk assessments at the basin/local level

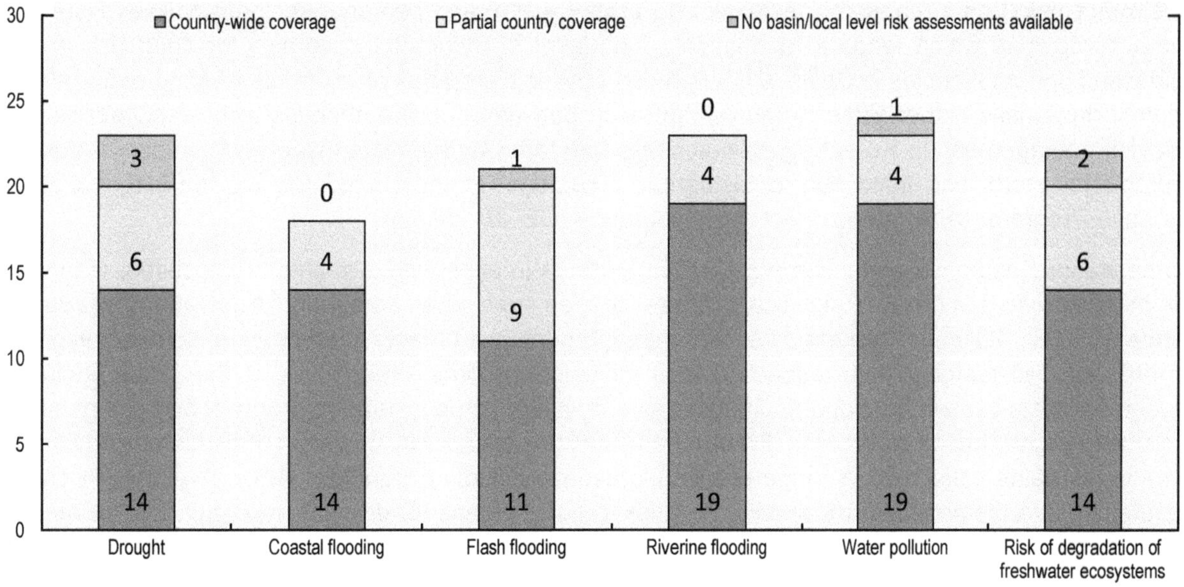

Note: Responses to question: "What is the coverage of risk assessments at the basin/local level?".
Source: 2019 survey on the implementation of the OECD Council Recommendation on Water; 27 responses received, including 26 Adherents.

Different institutions are responsible for conducting the risk assessments for different types of water related risks. In most Adherents, hydrometeorological hazards such as hurricanes, typhoons and river floods are not conducted by the same departments responsible for risks related to water-quality. Some countries like **Japan** and **Finland** have government departments that assess all water-related risks. In Ireland, Met Éireann (DHPLG) in collaboration with the Office of Public Works (OPW), which is lead agency for flood risk management, is currently establishing a National Flood Forecasting and Warnings Service to forecast for fluvial and coastal floods, and DHPLG would co-ordinate the response to larger flood events. The diversity of risk ownership for water related risks, even within the same institution, can lead to analytical silos. An identified good practice is for governments to conduct integrated approaches whereby one type of water related risk, such as a coastal or river flood, could also provoke a different type of water related risk, such as water pollution. Most Adherents now use all-hazards "National risk assessments" to promote a coordinated, whole of government approach to identify sequencing between different types of hazardous events. Several Adherents use these tools to inform decisions on prioritization of investments in disaster risk reduction (OECD, 2018[3]).

5.2.1. Financial protection strategies

A key use of risk assessment is to inform the design of financial protection strategies for water-related risks. Private insurance companies provide coverage both for flood damage and liability for water pollution. In most Adherents, insurance protection against flood risk is offered as an optional add-on to standard property policies, either as a single peril or in combination with other disaster risks. In **Japan** and **Turkey**, for example, flood coverage is included in standard residential property policies. In **Switzerland**, it is mandatory in 22 cantons to provide insurance coverage for residential and commercial buildings against a number of natural disasters. Flood insurance for residential properties has only recently become available in **Canada** and the **Netherlands** (OECD, 2016[5]).

In some Adherents, the public sector provides financial backing for the insurance coverage of flood risk, either as a direct insurer or as a reinsurer for properties. In France, reinsurance for all-natural disaster risks is provided by the Caisse central de réassurance (CCR) for up to 50% of the losses. In the case of Spain, the Consorcio de Compensación de Seguros (CCS) [1] provides direct insurance for flood (and other catastrophe risks) as a mandatory extension to property, life, and personal accident policies issued by private companies which leads to a relatively high-level of insurance coverage for flood risk among businesses and households in Spain. CCS is recognised in Europe as an example of good management of catastrophe risks that enables strong co-operation between public authorities with responsibilities for flood risk management. In Korea, a public scheme (operated by a private insurance company) provides coverage for storm and flood risk to residential properties. In the United States, the National Flood Insurance Program (NFIP) offers direct flood insurance (OECD, 2016[5]).

Compensation, insurance and income-smoothing policies to cope with droughts in agriculture is another area in which one can observe significant differences, as seen when comparing **Australia**, **Canada** and **France** (OECD, 2016[6]). **Canada** has risk management instruments that provide compensation for farmers' reduced margins, with respect to their individual records, irrespective of the cause, including reduced harvests caused by droughts. It also has a multi-peril crop insurance program that compensates for reduced yields caused by drought. **France** has a subsidised insurance system that indemnifies farmers for reduced yields caused by a range of climatic events including droughts. When available in certain countries, insurance provides risk-sharing and risk-transfer means for drought risks, but only for farmers relying on precipitation (rainfed). None of the three countries provides compensation for water shortages. In Canada, France, and to some extent **Australia** there are also instruments available to farmers to smooth their revenues across time as an element of the risk management toolbox. However, the design, policy mix, and degree of public support to these time smoothing instruments vary a great deal across countries: ex ante subsidised precautionary saving tools for risk management purpose (**Canada**, **France**); income tax smoothing schemes with or without subsidies (**Australia**, **Canada**, **France**); or ex post subsidised interest rates to refinance farms in circumstances of natural disaster (**Australia**, **France**) (OECD, 2016[6]).

5.3. Risk awareness

The Recommendation calls on Adherents to invest in "risk awareness of population, communities and business exposed or affected". Figure 5.4 shows that all respondents consider addressing the population at large to be a key action to raise awareness for water-related risks.

Figure 5.4. Actions to raise awareness of exposure to water-related risks

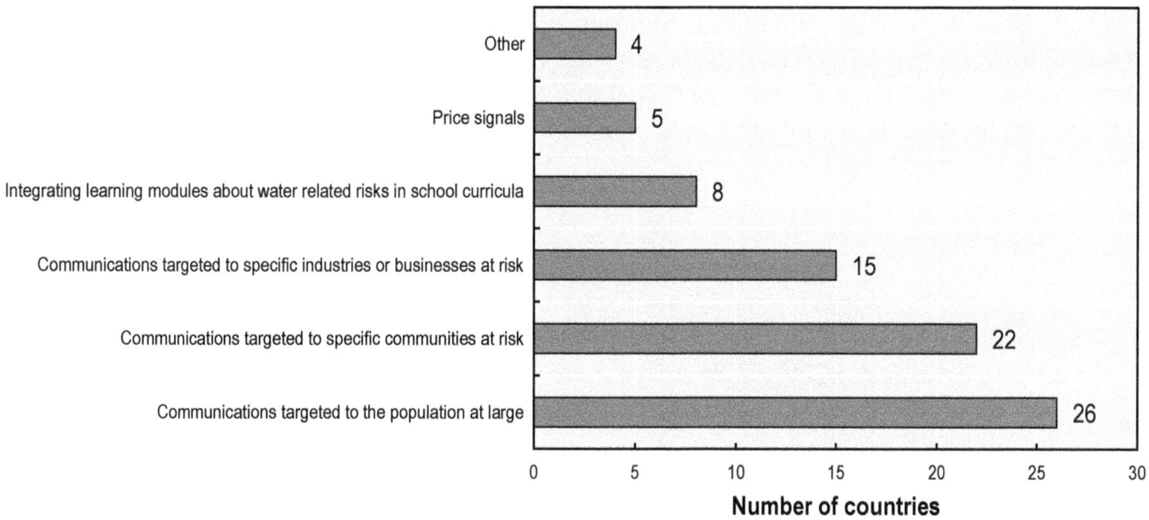

Note: Responses to question: "What actions has your country taken to raise awareness of exposure to water-related risks?". Multiple responses were possible.
Source: 2019 survey on the implementation of the OECD Council Recommendation on Water; 27 responses received, including 26 Adherents.

Based on the results of the 2019 OECD Implementation Survey, almost all responding Adherents communicate about risks with specific communities at risk, whereas 56% focus on industries or businesses at risk in order to minimise possible disruptions. Considerably less, only 30% of Adherents, integrate learning modules about water related risk in school curricula. This practice is followed in **Austria, Ireland, the Slovak Republic** and the **Republic of Korea**. Price signals, such as abstraction charges reflecting water scarcity risks, is implemented by less than 20% of Adherents.

Various types of flood risk awareness raising campaigns are implemented to more closely align risk perception with current scientific knowledge. In **the United Kingdom** residents can obtain by email the flooding history for any property based on Environment Agency records. This service is provided free of charge unless it takes more than 18 hours to compile. Efforts are being made to make scientific knowledge more accessible to the general public. In **France,** river festivals attended by tens of thousands include interactive games, cultural and historical presentations to increase public attention to flood risk information (OECD, 2014[7]).

The provision of flood hazard maps to exposed residents and businesses is a good practice to raise awareness of the population to water related risks. Yet, only 66% of Adherents reportedly make flood hazard maps available to the public (OECD, 2016[8]). Information about exposure to natural hazards is in some cases withheld to avoid volatility in real estate markets. In **Japan** local municipalities hand deliver flood hazard maps to households, which include directions to designated evacuation zones (OECD, 2009[9]).

Figure 5.5 shows that Adherents generally follow the good practice of joint responsibility for risk communication. Public authorities at the national level communicate about risks of national significance while local authorities tailor messages to local conditions. In **the Netherlands**[2], for example, the National Risk Profile is a publicly available document that aims to create a better understanding of all hazards and threats, including water related risks such as river and coastal floods, extreme weather and drought. The state, the water boards and the Delta programme share responsibility to inform citizens about the flood risk in the areas in which they live and work. A web tool enables users to enter a postal code to view its exposure to flood risk.

Adherents continue to distribute informative pamphlets to local residents to communicate about local risks. In **France**, for example, municipalities subject to a flood risk prevention plan (PPRi) are obliged to provide an information document on major risks (DICRIM) that presents a local hazard map and communicates safety measures to critical public infrastructure operators and residents (Ferrer, 2018[10]).

Figure 5.5. Actors with formal responsibilities for risk communication

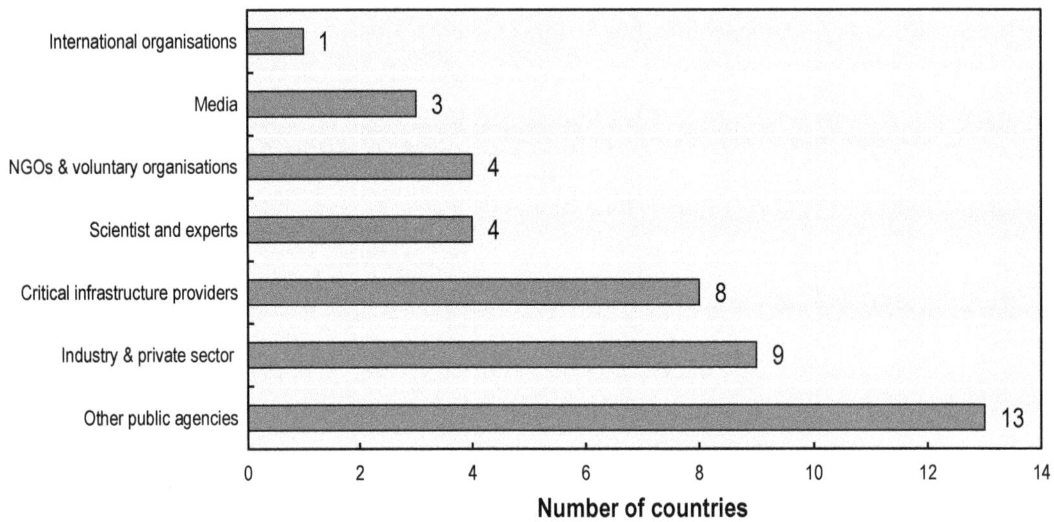

Note: Total number of responding countries: 19/19
Source: OECD Questionnaire on Risk Communication Policies and Practices, 2015

While Adherents have generally made risk communication a joint responsibility between national and sub-national governments, fewer than 50% of Adherents leverage the private sector and civil society organisations (OECD, 2016[8]) to raise awareness of water related risks. Additional efforts are still needed in most Adherents to achieve a whole of society approach to risk communication.

5.4. Setting and revising acceptable levels of water risk

The Recommendation encourages Adherents "setting, and regularly revising acceptable levels of water risks, that reflect societal values".

Targets for water risk reduction vary between uses of water. For example large dams might be built to resist a 1:1 000 year flood or probable maximum flood. Residences and major roads might be built to avoid inundation from a 1:100 year flood, while minor roads and recreational facilities might only be secured from a 1:10 year flood. Surprisingly, New York City is protected to only a 1-in-100-year flood event in comparison to other agglomerations such as London, Shanghai, or Amsterdam, all of which are protected to a greater than 1-in-1 000 year flood (Amsterdam is protected against a 1-in-10 000-year return floods).

Similarly, for water supplies, urban potable water might be provided at a service level to meet demand in 95% of years and not cause any human sickness in 99% of years; whilst high security irrigation water for permanent horticulture might only meet demand in 90% of years and have lower water quality requirements such as salinity levels; and low security water supplies for annual crops and pasture might only meet demand in 50% of years and have a higher threshold of tolerable salinity.

Environmental water requirements can also take a similar form of percentage risk. **Australian** red gum floodplain forests on the Murray River, for example, require flooding for one month or more in 70% of years, while drier floodplain woodland ecosystems only require flooding for two months or more in 25% of years. Each use of water thus has a different level of acceptable risk (in this case a risk of shortage for the ecosystems that require periodic flooding).

The Delta programme in the Netherlands is a government-led initiative to set the acceptable level of flood risk and drive investment and financing decisions to deliver that level of protection. The governance of the programme reflects the benefit of stakeholder engagement to set the acceptable level of risk (see chapter 6). Cost Benefit Analysis and Multi-Criteria Analysis provide useful information to evaluate water related disaster risk and to set acceptable levels of water risk (HELP, 2019[11]).

5.5. Prevention and mitigation measures

The Recommendation calls on Adherents to invest in "risk prevention and mitigation through a mix of structural protection measures (i.e. engineering or civil work prevention measures aimed at reducing exposure to hazards by protecting assets or communities, or controlling the variability of natural phenomena) and non-structural measures to prevent and reduce risks (including ecosystems based solutions and green infrastructures, when appropriate), and, where needed, the provision of incentives and tools to foster private self-protective and resilience building measures".

Figure 5.6 indicates that 85% of the respondents invest in structural protection measures like dikes, dams and waterways that protect riverine and coastal populations, and that public investments still dominate over private such investments. In some cases, public-private partnerships can be appropriate when risks and opportunities for revenues are shared in fair and appropriate ways between partners. The Thames Barrier (**United Kingdom**) is a good practice example of a public-private partnership financed protective infrastructure that holds back storm surges and high tides. The Thames Barrier helps protect 1.3 million people, USD 330 billion in property and infrastructure, and places of high historical and cultural value from flooding.

Figure 5.6. Actions to reduce water-related risks through prevention and mitigation measures

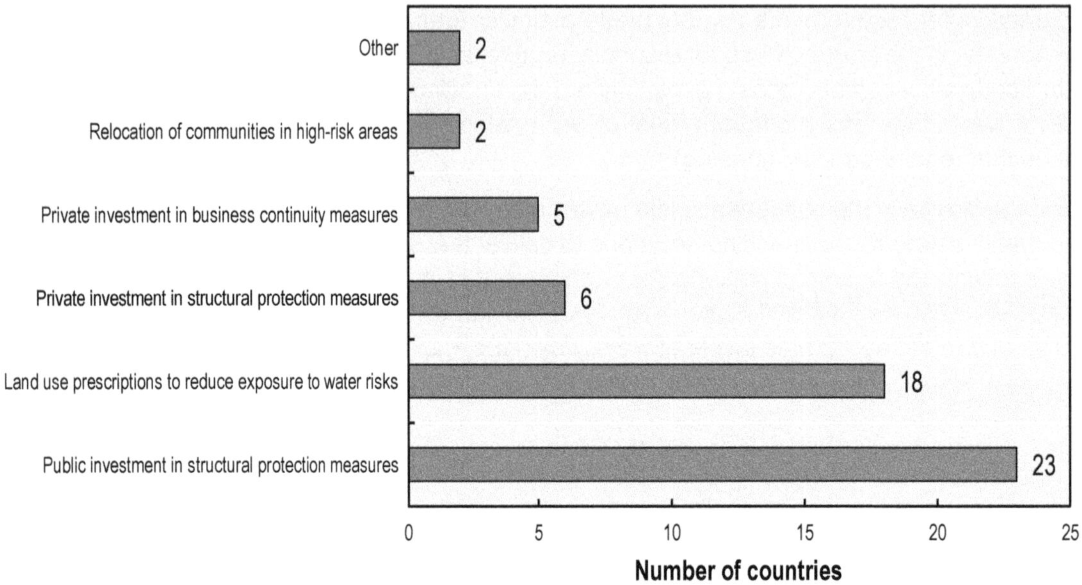

Note: Responses to the question: "What actions has your country taken to reduce water-related risks through prevention or mitigation measures?". Multiple responses were possible.
Source: 2019 survey on the implementation of the OECD Council Recommendation on Water; 27 responses received, including 26 Adherents.

Ecosystem-based approaches to flood management, such as upper watershed restoration and increasing green space in cities, can complement and in some cases replace structural protection measures. An increasing number of OECD countries are promoting the use of such approaches to manage flood risks (see Box 5.1). Some countries have enacted policy measures of financial support to encourage their use. In the **United States**, Army Corps of Engineers has streamlined the permitting process for the use of natural shorelines as coastal buffers, in an effort to incentivise these measures and correct the comparative advantage held by engineered infrastructure projects in terms of shorter time frames to receive permits (OECD, 2019[12]). In **Europe**, the EU Horizon 2020 framework programme for research and innovation, has allocated approximately EUR 185 million to research and pilot applications between 2014 and 2020 (European Parliament, 2017[13]).

Box 5.1. The use of ecosystem-based approaches to manage water-related risks

Countries are gaining more experience with using ecosystem-based approaches to manage water-related risks. The great majority of respondents to the 2019 survey on the implementation of the OECD Recommendation on Water confirm their countries include ecosystem-based approaches in national water management strategies. Both research and cases of early adoption have presented evidence of the multiple benefits of ecosystem-based approaches. For example, protecting coastal marshes can provide ecosystem services including flood abatement, carbon and nutrient sequestration, water quality maintenance, and habitat for fish, shellfish, wildlife and other flora. Green roofs and urban parks can be used to absorb floodwater and reduce temperatures, while providing recreational value and improving wellbeing.

While ecosystem-based approaches are being promoted in water management strategies, most implemented on the ground have been launched as pilot projects and at relatively small scale (a notable exception being the *Room for the River* programme in the **Netherlands**). Only 2 respondents to the 2019 survey found current implementation of ecosystem-based approaches to be absolutely adequate, whereas 17 saw room for improving implementation (Figure 5.7)

Figure 5.7. Level of awareness, technical capacity and implementation progress for NbS

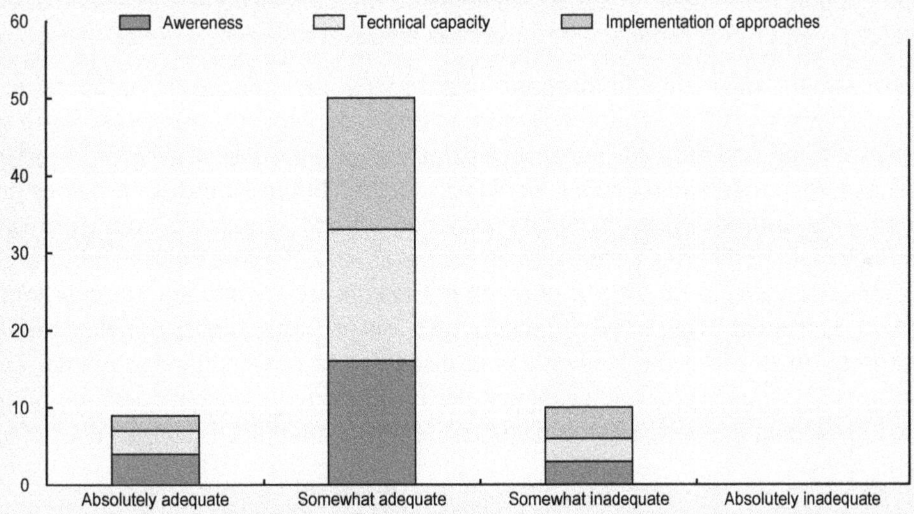

Note: Response to the question "How adequate are the following features in relation to eco-system-based approaches to water management in your country/basin?" Multiple responses were possible.
Source: 2019 survey on the implementation of the OECD Council Recommendation on Water; 27 responses received, including 26 Adherents.

70% of responding Adherents report the adoption of land use management as a tool in territorial planning to increase socio-economic resilience to water related risks. A good practice followed in several Adherents is to establish flood-vulnerability classifications of different types of developments and uses. The higher the economic value of a construction or use, such as transport, communication or energy infrastructure, the lower should be the flood hazard in the area where it is located. Inappropriate land-use development can have significant socio-economic impacts. In the **United States**, for example, high-risk properties accounted for 38% of all flood payment claims between 1978 and 2004 (OECD, 2016[5]).

As indicated in Figure 5.6, relocation of communities in high-risk areas is one possibility to correct for past land-use management decisions. After Hurricane Sandy hit New York, the state government implemented a buyout program to compensate homeowners with the full pre-storm market value of their properties. To mitigate against the possibility of community deterioration, the program offered a premium of 10% for residents that participated collectively in the program. In Australia, residents of the town Grantham were relocated to higher grounds through a voluntary land swap program following the deadly flash flooding in 2011 (OECD, 2016[5]).

Relatively few responding Adherents reported government sponsored programmes to promote private investment in business continuity measures in face of water related risks. Good examples can be found, for example in the Loire river basin in **France** where a dedicated programme provides a free vulnerability diagnosis of businesses to floods (OECD, 2017[14]).

Regarding the agricultural sector, 28 responding Adherents implemented policies to manage flood risks through a combination of mitigation and adaptation policies. For example, **Colombia, Costa Rica, Estonia, Italy, Latvia, New Zealand, Norway, Portugal** and **Spain** have developed national risk management frameworks specifically for flood, which include plans for agriculture sector. Other countries have different flood management tools such as hazard maps (**Japan** and **Poland**) and warning systems (**Japan**, **Korea** and **Turkey**). **France** and **Japan** use farmlands or rice paddy fields as a means to store and slow water to mitigate flood risks for urban areas.

Flood risks are also addressed indirectly by agriculture and water policies designed to fulfil other policy objectives. For instance, **Mexico, Poland** and **Portugal** support afforestation and restoration wetlands to slow water flows across agricultural land, which contribute to mitigate flood risks. **Finland, Hungary** and **Sweden** provide support for wetland that also indirectly contributes to flood mitigation. **Czech Republic** and **Norway**'s erosion and runoff reduction programmes also aim to reduce the risk of flooding.

24 Adherents implement payments to prepare and reduce the impact of droughts in agriculture. Programmes support practices that reduce soil erosion and retain soil moisture, reservoirs and irrigation facilities to conserve water, and farm advisory services as well as educational programmes for preparation of drought readiness, response and recovery. For instance, the **United Kingdom** provides grants to build up reservoirs, and the **United States** supports irrigation infrastructure, e.g. improved off-farm water conveyance technologies, to address water scarcity problems. In 2019 **Australia** established the National Water Grid Authority (NWGA) to develop a national framework for investment in water infrastructure to increase security and reliability of supply, funded through a mix of grants and loans. Increased international attention has been given to improve effectiveness of disaster risk reduction investments. The High-level Experts and Leaders Panel on Water and Disasters (HELP) provided practical guidance on the principles on investment and financing for water related disaster risk reduction (HELP, 2019[11]).

5.6. Emergency response measures

The Recommendation calls on Adherents to invest in "emergency response capabilities for both known hazards and threats as well as novel, unforeseen and complex events".

Based on the 2019 OECD Implementation Survey, Figure 5.8 shows that respondents have adopted a variety of emergency response measures that reflect the multi-dimensional nature of water-related risks. More than 90% of the respondents have put in place early warning systems for water related risks.

Figure 5.8. Emergency preparedness and response measures for water related risks

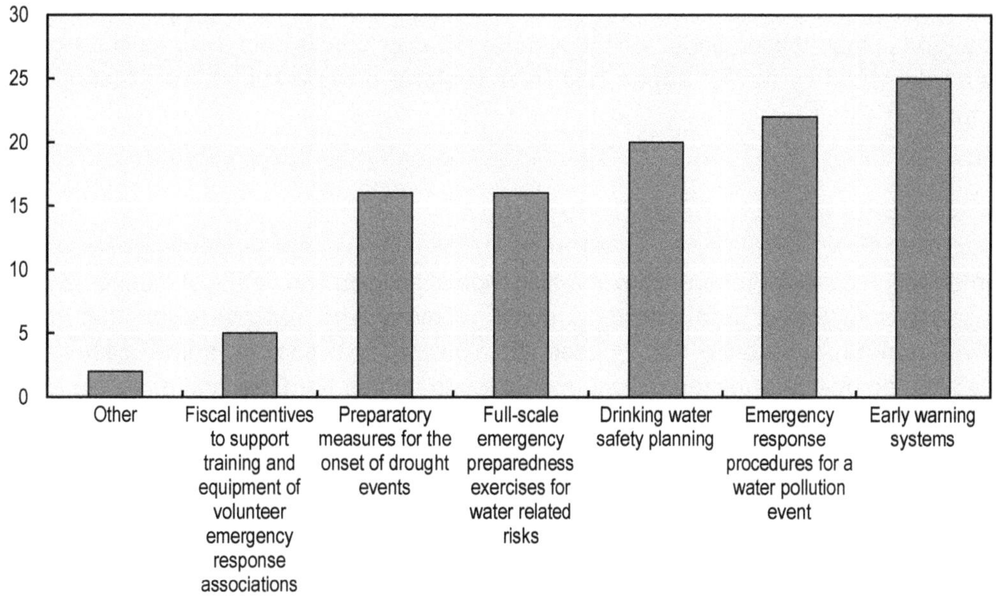

Note: Responses to the question: "What emergency response measures are in place for water-related risks?". Multiple responses were possible.
Source: 2019 survey on the implementation of the OECD Council Recommendation on Water; 27 responses received, including 26 Adherents.

Early warning systems provide crucial lead-time to exposed individuals and communities to take precautionary measures. In **France**, for example, the *Vigicrue* platform collects information on water levels in near real time and issues flood alerts for all river and major tributaries in the national territory. Since its inception, this system has gradually evolved to cover heavy rainfall warning and storm surge warnings. Warnings are widely disseminated through well-established partnerships with the media. Regular surveys demonstrated that the Vigilance map is known by 96 % of French citizens.

The **Japan** Meteorological Agency (JMA) develops flood forecasts and together with the Ministry of Land, Infrastructure, Transport and Tourism (MLIT) and prefectures works hand in hand to issue flood warnings. The **European** Flood Awareness System (EFAS) is the first operational European system that monitors and forecasts floods across Europe. It provides complementary, flood early warning information up to 10 days in advance to its partners including the National and Regional Hydrological Services as well as the Emergency Response and Coordination Centre of the European Commission. **Costa Rica, Korea** and **Turkey** also employ early flood warning systems for the farming sector. Across Adherents strong attention is also placed on emergency response to water pollution and drinking water safety. In **Austria**, **Finland**, **Sweden**, **Ireland** and the **Slovak Republic** the training and equipment of volunteer emergency response associations plays also a key role.

Conducting emergency response exercises further enables countries to spot weaknesses. The EU SEQUANA 2016 exercise in Ile-de-**France**, for example, aimed to test coordination between crisis management agencies in the event of a one-hundred-year flood of the River Seine, meaning an event with a 1% probability of occurring in any given year. The purpose of the exercise was to improve crisis management preparedness, but also to raise awareness among the population about the risks of a major flood.

In Italy, where floods are the most frequent type of natural hazard, the state provides fiscal advantages to certified volunteer civil protection organizations. These include tax breaks for the purchase of equipment, technical preparation and training to ensure the safety and security of volunteers. Salary refunds are also guaranteed to employers who allows certified volunteers to mobilize for rescues or trainings. In agriculture, disaster assistance programmes are available to affected farmers. Farmers in European Union countries can benefit from **EU** level and national disaster support when affected by droughts and floods. Farmers in **Israel** receive payments based on the Property Tax and Compensation Fund Regulation during declared drought years, and compensation based on the Natural Disaster Law is paid to agricultural infrastructures that have been damaged by floods. **Japan** and **New Zealand** provide support for clearing ground after major flooding.

5.7. Social policies and financial mechanisms

The Recommendation calls on Adherents to invest in "social policies and financial mechanisms to mitigate the welfare impacts of losses and ensure a quick recovery and reconstruction that reduce future vulnerability". Financial assistance for households, businesses and in some cases sub-national governments affected by water-related disasters enables to reduce hardship and minimize economic and social disruption.

Government compensation schemes are particularly present where flood risks are uninsurable. In the **Netherlands**, for example, the Calamities and Compensation Act enables the national government to compensate households impacted by freshwater flood events. The amount of compensation awarded to households is decided on a case-by-case basis, although the legislated aggregate of EUR 450 million cannot be exceeded. In the case of **Canada**, damages from overland flooding are usually excluded from residential insurance policies. The governments of Provinces and Territories may step in to provide financial assistance to households that have suffered from losses (OECD, 2016[5]).

Financial assistance and government compensation is also offered in Adherents where flood insurance is available. In **Belgium,** for example, affected businesses and households may approach the *Caisse nationale des Calamités*, if they consider the compensation of private insurance companies to be insufficient. Despite the absence of legal requirements in **Germany**, the Federal States have assisted households with damages incurred by past major flood events. The **United States**, in addition to providing subsidized flood insurance offers federal loans to homeowners (up to USD 200 000) and businesses to repair or replace damaged buildings (up to USD 2 million). These loans are available one time to all households and businesses affected by flood damages, although subsequent loans can only be granted, if the homeowner or business has secured flood insurance coverage (OECD, 2009[15]).

In **Austria,** the State budget provides for *Katfonds,* which cover up to 60 per cent of losses, and constitute the main source for financing mitigation measures. A lack of legal entitlement, however, leads to ambiguity and uncertainly concerning how much individual assistance the State will provide in any given case. It is conceivable that *KatFonds* might leave some affected citizens with low or no compensation at all (OECD, 2017[16])In France a public-private initiative funded by a surcharge on home insurance enables compensation for disaster damages, without drawing directly on a State budget. Each party has access to the insurance market and coverage against disasters under the constitutional principle of solidarity. (OECD, 2014[7]).

In addition to the losses households and businesses suffer from water-related disasters, central and sub-national governments incur costs of relief and recovery, reconstruction of public assets, as well as compensation and financial assistance. These expected costs are managed through public sector investments in cost-effective risk reduction measures. **Japan** exemplifies the efficiency that flood discharge works can offer. Following typhoon Ida in 1958, a single discharge channel was completed that lowered the Kano river water level around 1.85 meters. In 2019 typhoon Hagibis hit the same area at an even higher intensity, but no flooding was reported, resulting in estimated avoided damages of around US 7 billion.

5.8. Transparency, accountability and public awareness

The Recommendation calls on Adherents to invest in "transparency, accountability and public awareness in water risk related decision-making".

Transparency and access to hazard information on water risks is key to raising public awareness about local water related hazard exposures, and informing public debate on land use policy. It is also useful to contextualize public warnings, inform emergency response plans and support the accountability of public officials. Without access to accurate hazard information, public risk awareness is uninformed or misinformed, and disaster risk reduction measures undermined.

Access to water hazard data is needed to develop flood hazard maps, which are one tool to raise public risk awareness and inform prevention measures in urban planning. In **Switzerland** and the **United Kingdom** detailed hazard maps are made available on-line, for each canton and county. In **France**, municipalities subject to a 'Risk Prevention Plan' must provide accessible information including a map of hazardous areas within their jurisdiction to raise public awareness of risks.

Hazard data on specific geographic areas is the scientific basis for contentious land use decisions that may decrease or increase land values. Measures to support hazard data transparency are key to the credibility of these decisions. Good practices include multi-stakeholder platforms and commissions that can access the development of hazard plans and corroborate, or contest, the scientific basis for plans. In **Austria**, the process of adopting hazard maps includes public consultations, which are a crucial safeguard against bias (OECD, 2017[16]).

Accountability of public officials in the exercise of their duties to manage water related risks can support effective policy implementation. Good practices are found in **Austria** and **France** where local authorities may be held liable for damages occurring to persons and property, if they grant building permits in known flood zones (OECD, 2017[16]).

5.9. Policy coherence

The Recommendation calls on Adherents to "improve policy coherence across climate change adaptation, water management, land management, spatial planning, ecosystem and biodiversity protection and disaster risk reduction".

Policy coherence across climate change adaptation, water management, land management, spatial planning, ecosystem and biodiversity protection and disaster risk reduction is needed to identify both trade-offs and synergies between different areas (OECD, 2018[17]). For example, inappropriate land-use development can be a substantial driver of increased losses due to flooding (OECD, 2016[5]). Regulatory instruments such as spatial planning can reduce the exposure of new assets to water-related hazards, as well as reduce the impact of hazards by dedicating land to natural buffers and retention areas, such as wetlands. One illustration of a coherent approach between land use planning, disaster risk management and climate change adaptation is of **Ireland's** National Planning Framework, which contains specific policy objectives linked to adapting to sea-level rise (OECD, 2019[12]).

A survey of adaptation strategies across OECD countries (OECD, 2013[18]) suggested that, in the development of adaptation strategies or plans, water is nearly always addressed as a priority sector or cross-cutting theme vital for a number of key policy domains (e.g. energy, agriculture, infrastructure, biodiversity, and health). Climate change adaptation is also be being mainstreamed into existing water policies. Both approaches are important to ensure coherence and effectiveness.

5.10. Water risks related to climate change in agriculture

The Recommendation encourages Adherents to "take into account the specificities of water risks related to climate change for agriculture, in particular by fostering an enabling environment for adaptation of agriculture and water systems and by combining the dimensions and scales whereby climate, water and agriculture policies intersect".

The agricultural sector is particularly vulnerable to water-related risks and disasters (OECD, 2017[19]). Water related disasters have direct impacts on farmers, can generate losses of crop and livestock production, and damage to farmland, machinery or agricultural facilities. They can also result in indirect losses caused by interruptions to farm business activities.

The recent water related disasters illustrate this. **Japan**'s heavy rainstorms in 2018 triggered the deadliest floods since 1982, leading to damage valued at USD 3 billion for the agricultural sector (MAFF, 2019[20]).The heavy rain and flooding across the Midwestern **US** in 2019 cost several USD billions, washed up soils, and resulted in major delays in planting. Droughts also cause tremendous damage to the agriculture. The extreme drought event that affected Central and Northern Europe in 2018 resulted in cereals yields declining by up to 50% for certain crops. Some estimate that the US maize production losses may double during the next decades if the frequency of extreme rains and flooding were to increase, causing additional damages totalling an estimated USD 3 billion per year (Rosenzweig et al., 2002[21]).

With extreme weather events, including heavy precipitations, affecting the agricultural sector, most Adherents account for **climate change impacts** in their agriculture and water policies[3]. Almost all Adherents are engaged in public R&D efforts on climate change in agriculture and water. More specifically, a majority of Adherents are conducting assessments of regional impacts of precipitation and water availability, followed by analysis of climate change impact on agricultural production (Figure 5.9).

Figure 5.9. Focus of major public funded research related to water availability to agriculture

Number of Adherents conducting the respective public research, 2009-2019

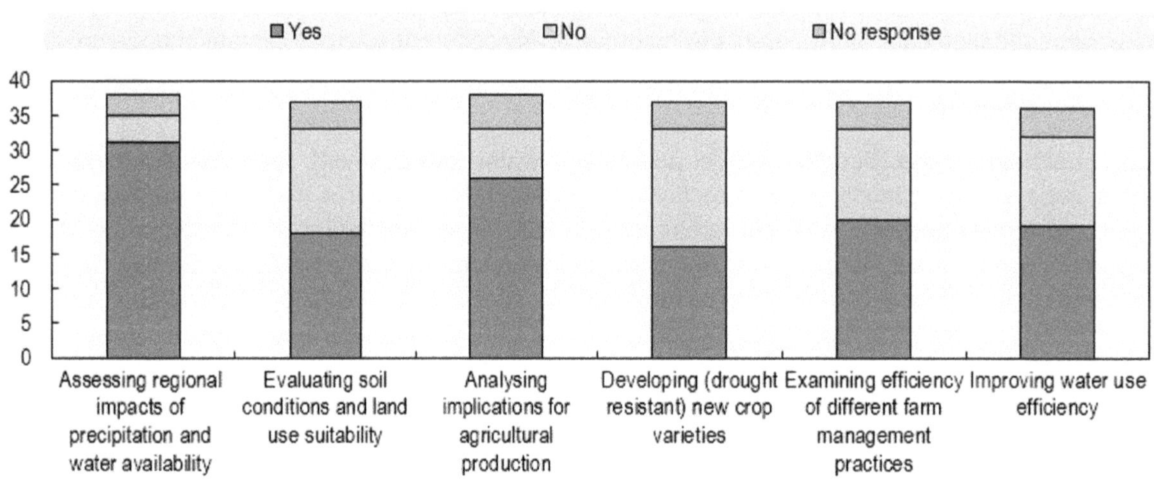

Source: (Gruère, Shigemitsu and Crawford, 2020[22])

Some Adherents have incorporated climate change considerations into their agriculture and water policy frameworks. For example, **Colombia** is formulating a Comprehensive Climate Change Management Plan for the Agricultural Sector in addition to establishing a Climate Change Law, the National Climate Change Adaptation Plan and the Adaptation Roadmap, **Latvia** has approved a Climate Change Adaptation Plan until 2030, which includes a specific section for agriculture. This plan includes seven agricultural measures and two measures related to water management. However, the degree of incorporation of climate change consideration into policies varies greatly across Adherents, probably commensurate with their respective projected impacts. Only 8 of responding Adherents reported an increase in the importance of climate change considerations in agriculture water management decisions from 2009 to 2019. The degree of considerations for climate change concerns remained unchanged in 13 of the Adherents during the last ten years (Gruère, Shigemitsu and Crawford, 2020[22]).

More generally, the results of the alignment analysis suggest that most Adherents, and especially relatively water abundant Adherents, still have progress to do to align their policies to manage water risks in agriculture with the OECD Council recommendation on Water, to adapt to climate change related water supply shocks (Gruère, Shigemitsu and Crawford, 2020[22]).

5.11. Water risks related to cities

The Recommendation calls on Adherents to "take into account the specificities of water risks related to cities, acknowledging that urban areas and their hinterland are interconnected through watersheds and groundwater systems, and, in particular use urban policies and infrastructure finance to promote water sensitive urban design".

As urban areas host approximately 50% of the global population (estimated to increase to 60% by 2050), ensuring good water governance in cities is crucial. Projections also show global water demand increasing by about 55% by 2050, leading to increased competition across water users, including agriculture, energy and urban dwellers. If cities remain in a business as usual outlook towards water governance, water risks of too much, too little and too polluted water will threaten their water security (OECD, 2016[23]). To respond, it is important to raise awareness among citizens and policy makers; engage with stakeholders, including property developers and long-term institutional investors, to build consensus on the acceptable level of risk and secure willingness to pay for water services; and strengthen water-related data and information for more robust early-warning systems, monitoring and evaluation. Good practices include the Bologna Local Urban Environment Adaptation Plan for a Resilient City (BLUEAP) in **Italy**, which involved 150 stakeholders, 70 project ideas and 6 pilot actions to come, amongst others, with solutions to water scarcity. The Water Observatory of the municipality of Paris, **France** provides a multi-stakeholder consultative platform prior to discussions at the City Council. Information and communications technologies are used to display water quality and quantity data in a number of cities including Marseille, **France**, while communication campaigns such as "Max 100" in Copenhagen, **Denmark** raised awareness of citizens and fostered water savings (OECD, 2016[23]).

The high quality of urban water services in OECD countries is threatened by an investment backlog impeding the upgrading, renewal and maintenance of water-related infrastructure. There is a need to address public investment issues including multilevel co-ordination and capacity challenges; foster cross-sectoral approaches to infrastructure; adopt an approach that encompasses multiple purposes; manage trade-offs across water users in rural and urban areas and between current and future generations in terms of who pays for what; and reduce investment needs by ensuring stable regulatory frameworks to catalyse finance and enhance efficiency. Financial tools will also be needed to support the digital transformation in the water sector, mainly for municipal water supply systems. Similarly, they will be needed for climate change adaptation measures to boost cities' resilience, for example, against floods or re-naturalisation management of green urban areas. In the **United States**, the EPA Water Infrastructure and Resiliency Finance Centre set up in April 2015 to help US municipalities efficiently use federal and local funds for water infrastructure, explore financing options and showcase best practices (OECD, 2016[23]).

Water in cities is affected by decisions taken in other sectors and vice versa, in particular agriculture, energy, finance, solid waste, transport and land use. There is a need to ensure that water is recognised as a key factor of sustainable growth in cities. Such a strategic vision is essential for strengthening policy coherence for an integrated urban water policy, mitigating split incentives whereby those generating future liabilities do not bear related costs, and fostering a whole-of-government approach that builds on horizontal and vertical co-ordination. For instance, in the **Netherlands** "water assessments" are carried out in municipalities to factor in water-related stakes and costs in spatial planning decisions; the city of Cologne, **Germany** co-ordinates water and spatial planning for new building areas to prevent flood damages because of heavy rainfalls; in France, Eau de Paris put in place concrete actions to promote organic agriculture for the preservation of water and natural resources through signing contracts with farmers associations (OECD, 2016[23]).

Water boundaries cut across administrative perimeters. Multi-level approaches are needed from basin to local levels depending on the water function (protection against floods or droughts, water supply, sanitation, drainage, etc.). A functional approach is key to addressing linkages between urban areas (where most people live) and the surrounding environments (rural and watersheds) that sustain them. This would also help optimise the opportunity cost of investments and the efficient use of water. Rural-urban partnerships should be seen as win-win-win solutions, benefiting cities, upstream and downstream communities and ecosystems. Good practices include multi-stakeholder committees such as the technical committee created in Montreal, **Canada,** composed of representatives from community organisations, the industrial sector, government departments, other levels of government and municipal services, to improve the quality of discharged water in catchment areas. Other practices include contracts between the Utility and watershed communities to preserve both water quality and the economic dynamism as in the case of New York City, **United States** (OECD, 2016[23]).

References

European Parliament (2017), *Nature-based solutions: Concept, opportunities and challenges*, http://www.europarl.europa.eu/thinktank/en/document.html?reference=EPRS_BRI(2017)608796 (accessed on 29 October 2019). [13]

Ferrer, L. (2018), *Analysis of a risk prevention document using dependdability techniques: a frist step towards an effectiveness model*. [10]

Gruère, G., M. Shigemitsu and S. Crawford (2020), "Agriculture and water policy changes: Stocktaking and alignment with OECD and G20 recommendations", *OECD Food, Agriculture and Fisheries Papers*, No. 144, OECD Publishing, Paris, https://dx.doi.org/10.1787/f35e64af-en. [22]

HELP (2019), *Principles on Investment and Financing for Water-related Disaster Risk Reduction*, https://www.mlit.go.jp/common/001295211.pdf. [11]

MAFF (2019), *Annual Report on Food, Agriculture and Rural Area in Japan FY 2018 (in Japanese)*. [20]

OECD (2019), *Applying the OECD Principles on Water Governance to Floods: A Checklist for Action*, OECD Studies on Water, OECD Publishing, Paris, https://dx.doi.org/10.1787/d5098392-en. [1]

OECD (2019), *Responding to Rising Seas: OECD Country Approaches to Tackling Coastal Risks*, OECD Publishing, Paris, https://dx.doi.org/10.1787/9789264312487-en. [12]

OECD (2018), *National Risk Assessments: A Cross Country Perspective*, OECD Publishing, Paris, https://dx.doi.org/10.1787/9789264287532-en. [3]

OECD (2018), *Policy Coherence for Sustainable Development 2018: Towards Sustainable and Resilient Societies*, OECD Publishing, Paris, https://dx.doi.org/10.1787/9789264301061-4-en. [17]

OECD (2017), *Boosting Disaster Risk Prevention through Innovative Risk Governance: Insights from Austria, France and Switzerland*. [16]

OECD (2017), *OECD Toolkit for Risk Governance: Program to reduce business vulnerability to floods in Loire basin (France)*, https://www.oecd.org/governance/toolkit-on-risk-governance/goodpractices/page/businessvulnerabilityreductiontofloodprogrammeintheloirebasin.htm# (accessed on 14 February 2020). [14]

OECD (2017), *Water Risk Hotspots for Agriculture*, OECD Studies on Water, OECD Publishing, Paris, http://dx.doi.org/10.1787/22245081. [19]

OECD (2016), *Financial Management of Flood Risk*, OECD Publishing, Paris, https://dx.doi.org/10.1787/9789264257689-en. [5]

OECD (2016), *Mitigating Droughts and Floods in Agriculture: Policy Lessons and Approaches*, OECD Studies on Water, OECD Publishing, Paris, https://dx.doi.org/10.1787/9789264246744-en. [6]

OECD (2016), *OECD Council Recommendation on Water*, https://www.oecd.org/environment/resources/Council-Recommendation-on-water.pdf. [2]

OECD (2016), *Trends in Risk Communication Policies and Practices*, OECD Reviews of Risk Management Policies, OECD Publishing, Paris, https://dx.doi.org/10.1787/9789264260467-en. [8]

OECD (2016), *Water Governance in Cities*, OECD Studies on Water, OECD Publishing, Paris, https://dx.doi.org/10.1787/9789264251090-en. [23]

OECD (2014), *Seine Basin, Île-de-France, 2014: Resilience to Major Floods*, OECD Publishing, https://doi.org/10.1787/9789264208728-en. [7]

OECD (2013), *Water and Climate Change Adaptation: Policies to Navigate Uncharted Waters*, OECD Studies on Water, OECD Publishing, Paris, https://dx.doi.org/10.1787/9789264200449-en. [18]

OECD (2009), *OECD Reviews of Risk Management Policies: Japan 2009: Large-Scale Floods and Earthquakes*, OECD Reviews of Risk Management Policies, OECD Publishing, Paris, https://dx.doi.org/10.1787/9789264050303-en. [9]

OECD (2009), *OECD Reviews of Risk Management Policies: Japan 2009: Large-Scale Floods and Earthquakes*, OECD Reviews of Risk Management Policies, OECD Publishing, Paris, https://dx.doi.org/10.1787/9789264050303-en. [15]

Rosenzweig, C. et al. (2002), "Increased crop damage in the US from excess precipitation", *Global Environmental Change*, Vol. 12, pp. 197–202. [21]

UK Environment Agency (2009), *Flooding in England: A National Assessment of Flood Risk*. [4]

Notes

1 www.consorseguros.es/web/inicio

2 www.overstroomik.nl

3 2019 OECD Survey on water and agriculture policy changes.

6. Ensuring good water governance

This chapter presents progress made by Adherents with water governance, in line with the OECD Recommendation on Water and the OECD Principles on water governance. The chapter explores how Adherents allocate and distinguish roles and responsibilities, and manage water at the appropriate scale(s). It highlights how policy coherence and effective cross sectoral co-ordination can be arranged. It illustrates how capacity can be adjusted to the complexity of water challenges. It also explores the use of data and information to guide policy. It illustrates how to efficiently mobilise finance for water governance, while promoting innovative water governance practices and mainstreaming integrity and transparency. The chapter focuses on promoting stakeholders engagement, managing governance complexity and trade-offs. Finally, it describes monitoring and evaluating mechanisms for water policy and governance.

The Recommendation calls on Adherents to "enhance the effectiveness and efficiency of, and trust and engagement in, water governance, taking into account the specificities of governance for groundwater management". Section 6 of the Recommendation reflects the OECD Principles on Water Governance, welcomed by Ministers at the 2015 meeting of the Council at Ministerial level [C/MIN(2015)12].

To support the implementation of section 6 of the Recommendation, three main actions have taken place. First, the OECD has provided translations of the Principles into 18 languages, all available online[1]. Second, the RDPC and its Water Governance Initiative (WGI) have produced water governance indicators, composed of a self-assessment framework piloted in 11 cities, basins or countries and a Checklist. Third, 50+ water governance stories were collected and analysed as "evolving practices" to draw lessons and shape best practices.

Box 6.1. OECD Principles on Water Governance

The OECD Principles on Water Governance intend to contribute to tangible and outcome-oriented public policies, based on three mutually reinforcing and complementary dimensions of water governance (Figure 6.1):

- *Effectiveness* relates to the contribution of governance to define clear sustainable water policy goals and targets at all levels of government, to implement those policy goals, and to meet expected targets.
- *Efficiency* relates to the contribution of governance to maximise the benefits of sustainable water management and welfare at the least cost to society.
- *Trust and Engagement* relate to the contribution of governance to building public confidence and ensuring inclusiveness of stakeholders through democratic legitimacy and fairness for society at large.

Figure 6.1. Overview of OECD Principles on Water Governance

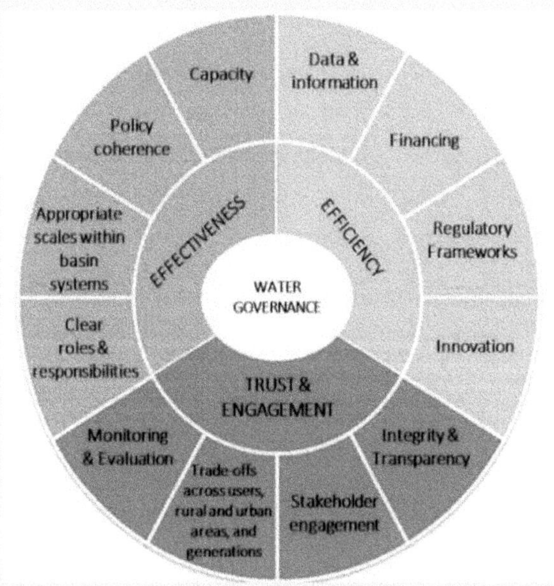

Source: *OECD Principles on Water Governance*, OECD, 2015. https://www.oecd.org/cfe/regional-policy/OECD-Principles-on-Water-Governance.pdf

To support the implementation of the OECD Water Governance Principles, three years after their adoption, two tools were developed Based on an extensive bottom up and multi-stakeholder process within the OECD Water Governance Initiative (WGI): a water governance indicator framework and a set of evolving practices for bench-learning, building on lessons learned from different countries and contexts.

The OECD Water Governance Indicator Framework aims support self-assessment at local, basin or national scale of governance frameworks (what), institutions (who) and instruments (how), and their needed improvements over time. The OECD Water Governance Indicator Framework (Figure 6.2) is composed of a Traffic light system of 36 water governance indicators (input and process) and a Checklist of 100+ questions. Its use results in the design of an Action Plan to improve water governance over the short, medium and long run. The Framework was pilot-tested by institutions at different scales and in different geographic and socio-economic contexts: **Austria, Cabo Verde, Peru, Scotland, United Kingdom, Netherlands, Peru, Spain, Morocco, Malaysia, Spain, Colombia and Democratic Republic of Congo**.

Figure 6.2. The OECD Water Governance Indicator Framework

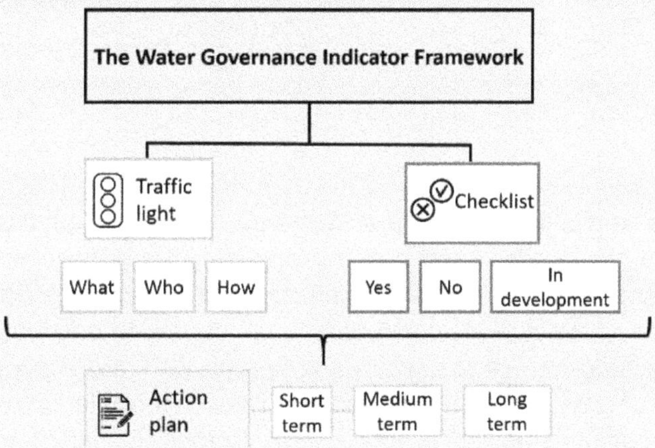

Source: (OECD, 2018[1])

The ten-step assessment (Figure 6.3) provides guidance for carrying out the self-assessment in the preparation phase, during the assessment (diagnosis) and after the assessment (actions). The self-assessment is a tool for dialogue among stakeholders to understand whether existing water institutions, policies and governance instruments are performing well or need adjustments. The self-assessment should occur through multi-stakeholder workshops to assess the water governance system against the traffic light and the checklist, and design the Action Plan. The action phase consists of linking actions with existing policy frameworks, strategies and plans; setting up an accountability process to track progress over time and keeping the dialogue alive; and considering repeating the self-assessment every three years (OECD, 2018[1]).

Figure 6.3. A ten-step assessment framework

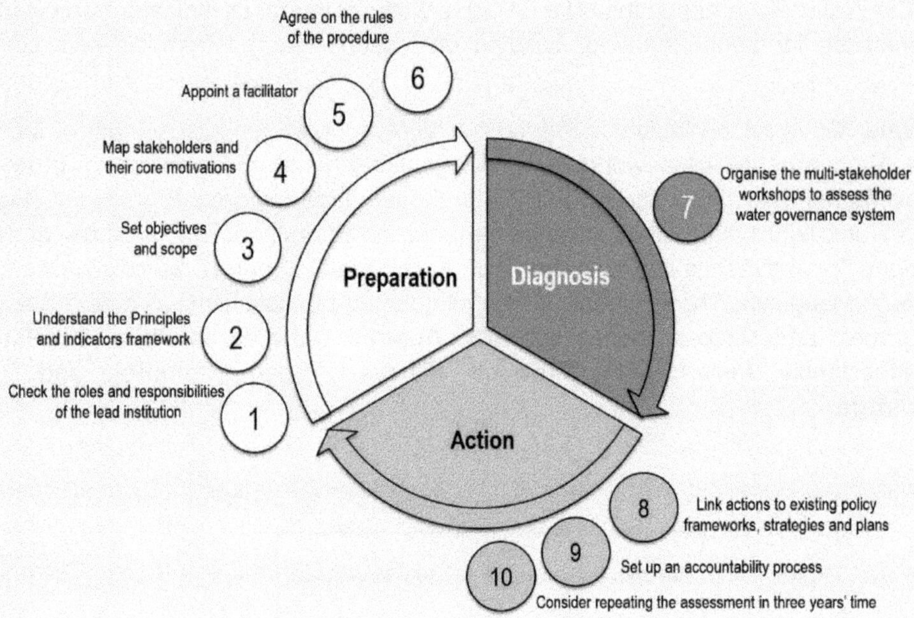

Source: (OECD, 2018[1])

The 54 *Evolving practices* help policy makers, practitioners and other stakeholders learn from each other and identify pitfalls to avoid when designing and implementing water policies. They were collected to provide examples and lessons that can inspire ambitious reforms and better policies and practices. At least 70% of the examples relate to "water resources" and "sanitation and water quality", close to 60% of the practices deal with "drinking water supply" and around 30% are associated with "water-related disasters". Most of the examples (45 evolving practices) refer to multiple water functions. The evolving practices cover the five continents (America, Africa, Asia, Europe, Oceania) with more than half (52%) of the practices from the European Union (Figure 6.4).

Figure 6.4. Map of the pilots and evolving practices

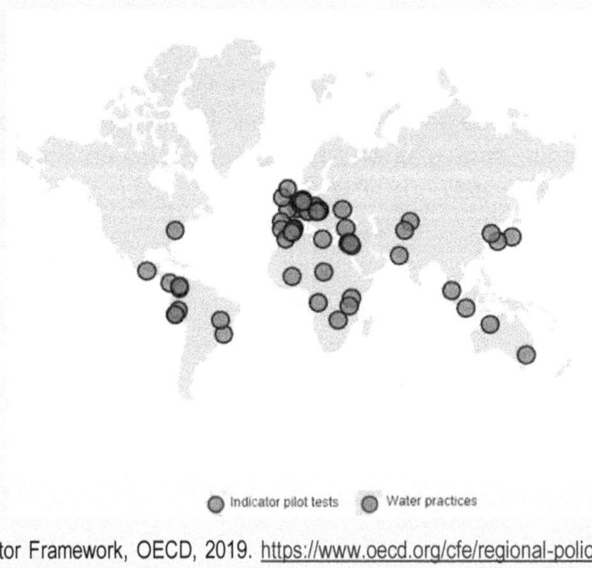

Source: The OECD Water Indicator Framework, OECD, 2019. https://www.oecd.org/cfe/regional-policy/oecd-water-governance-indicator-framework.htm

6.1. Clearly allocate and distinguish roles and responsibilities

The Recommendation asks Adherents to "clearly allocate and distinguish roles and responsibilities for water policymaking, policy implementation, operational management and regulation, and foster coordination across these responsible authorities".

In all Adherents, regardless of constitutional and institutional settings, water management is fragmented across multiple actors and sectors.

Many Adherents have engaged important reforms to coordinate and/or clarify roles and responsibilities. For instance, **Ireland** implemented a water governance reform that gives distinct responsibilities to three different tiers of government. In the first tier, the Department of Housing, Planning and Local Government is in charge of water policy and legislation; in the second, the Environmental Protection Agency is responsible for scientific research and responses, then reporting the evidence to other agencies; in the third, local authorities are in charge of local implementation and public engagement (OECD, 2018[1]). A multi-level governance approach based on sound coordination mechanisms can also minimise misalignments, complexity and overlaps for specific water functions. For instance, the Joint Flood Commission in **France** brings together the Steering Council for major natural risks prevention and the National Water Committee to co-ordinate flood management across levels of government and stakeholders from civil and environmental protection, urban planning and land-use (OECD, 2019[2]). In **Poland,** the Water Law of 2017 introduced a new structure for water administration bodies. Starting in 2018, the State Water Holding 'Polish Waters' is in charge of water management, with water resource decisions devolved to 11 Regional Water Management Authorities (which are regional units of Polish Water), and the responsibility to apply 50 water basin units and 330 water inspections (the most disaggregated entities of Polish Water).[2]

The multiplicity of actors varies according to the area of water policy considered. For example, in **Mexico**, municipalities are responsible for providing water and sanitation directly or indirectly. They can also delegate responsibility to private operators or utilities owned and operated by the state government. In the **Netherlands**, there are 21 regional water authorities that manage regional water systems to maintain water levels, water quality and wastewater treatment. These regional water authorities are decentralised public authorities that are endowed with specific legal personality and financial resources (OECD, 2014[3]). Additionally, the Administrative Agreement on Water Affairs signed in 2011 in the **Netherlands** between the Ministry of Infrastructure and Water Management, regional water authorities, drinking water companies, provinces and municipalities, aimed to foster efficiency gains across the water chain up to EUR 750 million per year until 2020 through improved collaboration and reallocation of roles and responsibilities (OECD, 2015[4]).

Decentralisation of water policies in the past decades has resulted in allocating increasingly complex and resource-intensive competences to subnational governments. According to the 2016 OECD Survey across 48 cities[3], in terms of policymaking, the role of local governments compared to other subnational actors is definitely predominant for drainage (67%), drinking water supply (56%), water security (56%) and sewage collection (52%). With no exception across water functions, the majority of cities indicated that local governments are the main actors providing information and carrying out monitoring and evaluation. This is particularly true for drinking water supply (58%). Compared to the responses attributed to central governments and to other subnational governments, the highest share of responses was attributed to local governments for financing related to drainage (58%); water security and drinking water (48%); sewage collection (46%); and wastewater treatment (40%) (OECD, 2016[5]).

6.2. Manage water at the appropriate scale(s)

The Recommendation asks Adherents to **"**manage water at the appropriate scale(s) within integrated basin governance systems to reflect local conditions, and foster co-ordination between the different scales**"**.

Water is a field particularly sensitive to issues of scale. Water logics and hydrological boundaries cut across administrative frontiers and perimeters. Water services and resources management take place at various spatial scales, both in their ecological and political dimensions.

In the **European Union**, the 2000 Water Framework Directive (WFD) emphasises the importance of management at the basin scale and the introduction of River Basin Districts, designated not according to administrative or political boundaries, but according to the spatial catchment area of the river as a natural geographical and hydrological unit. To implement the WFD, most EU member states have set up or strengthened dedicated river basin organisations, which in some cases have long existed, as in **France** (6 water agencies[4]). In **Spain**, river basin councils "*confederaciónes hidrográficas*", are deconcentrated authorities of the Ministry for the Ecologic Transition and the Demographic Challenge with the responsibility to manage river basins shared by more than one autonomous region. In addition, each basin counts with a council in which the governments of the autonomous regions participate. The river basin councils discuss river basin plans prepared by the "*confederaciónes hidrográficas*" before their adoption by the Council of Ministers following consultation of the National Water Council (OECD, 2015[4]). There are also other key bodies that complete the water governance system in each river basin district such as the Committees of Competent Authorities and the Water Councils. The **Netherlands**' approach to the WFD relies on seven basin level bodies governed by administrators in the provinces, regional water authorities and municipalities. These authorities, responsible for organising public participation, established "feedback groups" comprised of representatives of both interest groups and landowners, to reflect and comment on the river basin management plans at the appropriate scale. Individual water boards were also set up to discussregional goals and measures under an advisory status (OECD, 2014[3]). In **Germany**, the *Länder* are mainly responsible for the implementation of water legislation, and generally delegate many practical tasks of water management to local administrative bodies. They have to build consensus about shared river basins, namely in the process of preparing river basin plans. In some cases, like in the Ruhr River basin, there are users' associations with delegated powers promoting a consistent basin approach. The framework legislation on water corresponds to the federal level (*Bundestag,* federal government), however with several areas open for specific regulations by the *Länder*. The legal situation is often described as "competing legislation". The federal government is also responsible for international conventions on transboundary rivers (such as the Rhine, the Danube, the Odra or the Elbe) (OECD, 2015[4]). Basin level governance in other regions is equally as important.

Other Adherents, such as **Austria**, which counts three large transboundary river basins, alternatively approached basin governance, following instead a catchment-oriented governance to ensure co-ordination and co-operation at the basin level. The Austrian Water Act entrusts the Federal Ministry as the lead institution to design and implement river basin and flood risk management plans. The different actions that feature in the programme of measures are assigned to the authority according to the scale of intervention (OECD, 2018[1]).

Mexico has also been a pioneer among Latin American Adherents in river basin governance; the country first developed river basin commissions in the 1940s as the first implementing agencies of water-based development plans in the country. After the 1992 National Water Law, Mexico created 13 different river basin organisations based on regional hydrology. Thus, policies are implemented in accordance with the needs of each hydrographic region as implemented by the appropriate river basin organisation (OECD, 2013[6]).

Groundwater management is often an area where decentralised decisions will be the most effective. For instance, the **US State of Nebraska**, which was able to manage groundwater based irrigation effectively, relies on local management policies set up by Natural Resource Districts (OECD, 2015[7]). The **US States of Kansas and Texas** have also relied on similar local agencies, named Groundwater Management Districts (GMDs) and Groundwater Conservation Districts (GCDs), respectively (Ibid.).

A scale-sensitive governance approach can also minimise misalignments, complexity and overlaps for specific water functions. Specifically, river basin organisations or catchment-oriented institutions have an important role to play as intermediaries for inter-municipal or regional flood cooperation as exemplified by the work of river committees in Wallonia (**Belgium**) and the expansion of the scope of municipal flood management in **France** (OECD, 2019[2]).

6.3. Encourage policy coherence and effective cross-sectoral co-ordination

The Recommendation asks Adherents to **"**encourage policy coherence through effective cross-sectoral co-ordination, especially between policies for water and the environment, health, energy, agriculture, industry, spatial planning and land use**"**.

Policies in areas such as energy, agriculture, land use, territorial development, health, public works/infrastructure, economy and finance can have a significant impact on the economic, social and environmental sustainability of the water sector, which requires effective horizontal coordination and policy coherence. However, in practice, because of the sectoral fragmentation of water-related tasks across ministries and public agencies, policy makers constantly face conflicting objectives and the temptation of retreating into silo approaches.

Policy coherence is essential if governments wish to meet the range of sectoral policy goals without undermining the sustainability of the water resource base. Better water governance is critical to fostering inter-institutional mechanisms for horizontal co-ordination and encouraging synergies and complementarities between different policy fields related to water. Most Adherents have made important efforts to co-ordinate water with other policy areas, especially spatial planning, regional development, agriculture and energy; and to enhance integrated national strategic planning. For example, the 2018 integrated Environmental Planning Act in the **Netherlands** replaced and superseded all strategic plans, and was jointly developed by the central government and provinces to better align spatial planning, the environment, water, landscape, agriculture, cultural heritage and energy infrastructure. In **Portugal**, the long-term National Energy Strategy is jointly prepared by Ministry of Economy and the Ministry of the Environment and Land Use Planning; in **France**, the master plans of development and water management (*Schéma directeur d'aménagement et de gestion des eaux*, SDAGE) facilitate the co-ordination of hydropower operations and conservation of aquatic environments (OECD, 2015[4]). They are also legally binding for a large number of sectoral development plans such as the *Plan local d'urbanisme*, the *Schéma de cohérence territoriale*. In **Ireland**, co-ordinating committees ensure policy coherence across national authorities responsible for water, environmental and agricultural policies. In addition, the Water Policy Advisory Committee established in 2014 is chaired by the Department of Housing, Planning and Local Government, but also involves the Department of Agriculture, Food and the Marine to coordinate with the Rural Development Programme (OECD, 2018[1]). In **Korea**, in accordance with the Framework Act on Water Management, the Presidential Water Commission, involving heads of 8 ministries related to water management including the Ministry of Environment, fostered policy coherence and cross-sectoral coordination (Republic of Korea, 2020[8]).

In recent years, particular engagements have been taken and efforts have been undertaken to coordinate water and agriculture policies. In 2017 agriculture ministers of the G20 committed to actions to improve the use of water in agriculture, including to encourage the coherence of their policies in this area (Gruère, Ashley and Cadilhon, 2018[9]). The same year the European Commission reinitiated efforts to coordinate efforts on water and agriculture via the Taskforce on water and agriculture, considering progress to be made on both policy sides, organising three thematic workshops, setting a knowledge hub on agriculture and water, and developing a tool for better nutrient management at farm levels. The 2019 Implementation Survey also revealed that 21 respondents had made efforts to improve the coherence of agriculture and water policies (Figure 6.5).[5]

Figure 6.5. Coherence between water management and other sectoral plans

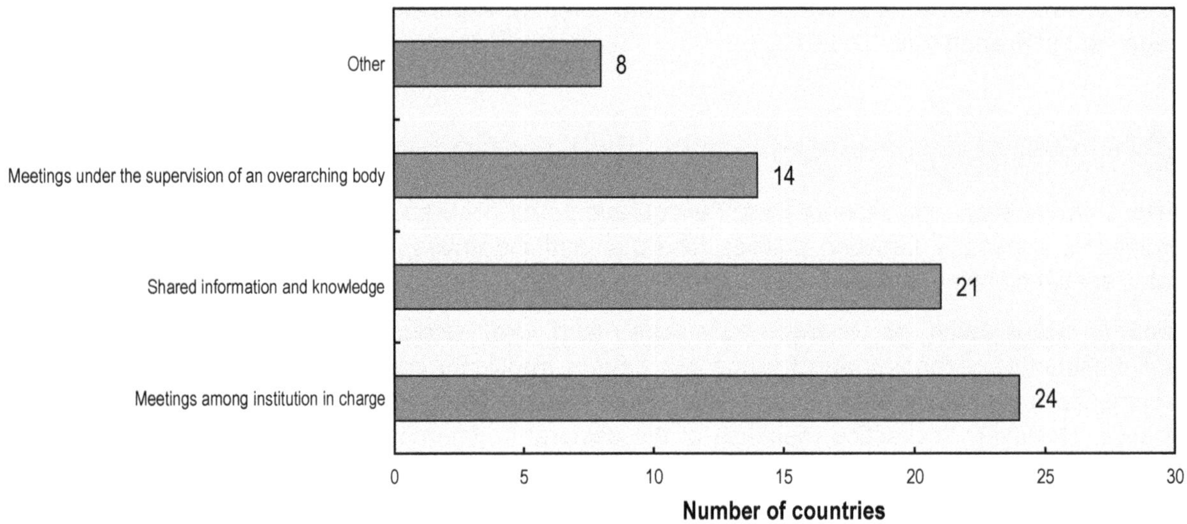

Note: Responses to the question: "How does your country ensure coherence between water management and other sectoral plans such as agriculture, land use and urban development, or energy?". Multiple responses were possible.
Source: 2019 survey on the implementation of the OECD Council Recommendation on Water; 27 responses received, including 26 Adherents.

Achieving policy complementarities means fostering an overall strategic approach across water policies and those related to them. For instance, in **Mexico**, the National Water Commission (CONAGUA)'s Technical Council is in charge of co-ordinating water policies and defining common strategies across multiple ministries and agencies (SEMARNAT; SEDESOL; Secretary of Agriculture, Livestock, Rural Development, Fisheries and Food [SAGARPA]; Treasury; Energy; CONAFOR; and IMTA) (OECD, 2015[4]). **France** created the Inter-ministerial Committee for Sustainable Development by decree in 2003. This committee gathers annually and consists of the ministers responsible for interior affairs, social affairs, employment, foreign affairs, European affairs, defence, youth, education, research, economy, finances, industry, transport, housing, tourism, health, agriculture, culture, state reform, territorial development, cities and local communities, sports and overseas territories. The committee prepares an annual evaluation report on the implementation of the strategy and actions plans (OECD, 2015[4]).

6.4. Adapt the level of capacity to the complexity of water challenges

The Recommendation asks Adherents to "adapt the level of capacity of responsible authorities to the complexity of water challenges to be met, and to the set of competencies required to carry out their duties."

The development of skills, technical expertise and knowledge and the availability of staff and time are preconditions for effective governance of water policy. In particular, in a context of decentralisation of water policy, governments face a fundamental question whether the sub-national level is ready or sufficiently mature to assume responsibilities associated with devoted or decentralised tasks. Any mismatch between the capacity needed to shoulder water responsibilities, and the organisational, technical, procedural, networking and infrastructure capacity of responsible authorities, will bear consequences for the implementation of national water policies. Institutional strengthening and capacity building at all levels are crucial for future-proof water policies.

To tackle issues related to capacity gaps, Flanders (**Belgium**) started to conduct water scans of local administrations as one of the key elements of the their projects for a rational water use in buildings as a stepping stone towards water wise cities aiming to achieve a 30% reduction of water consumption. The project is driving a structural reform to adapt the competence profiles of technicians to the capacity gaps identified in the local administration (OECD, 2018[1]). In **Ireland**, as a response to capacity challenges for policy implementation at the local level, the creation of a Catchment Management and Science Unit strengthened the knowledge base for river basin management and helped target resources appropriately (OECD, 2018[1]). In 2017, in **Australia**, the Council of Australian Governments (CoAG) published training modules of the National Water Initiative (NWI) on 'Considering climate change and extreme events in water planning and management' and 'Engaging Indigenous peoples in water planning and management'. Reviews of the NWI are required to assess progress against NWI objectives and commitments. The most recent review acknowledged the importance of maintaining the momentum where capacity is building in water reform, particularly in areas of urban water, Indigenous water interests, and management of environmental water (OECD, 2019[10]).

In the water sector, capacity building concerns both "hard" and "soft" capacity. There is a growing awareness that facilities, resources and inputs alone will not lead to lasting improvements in water governance performance. The typical "hard" capacities generally focused on facilities, equipment and infrastructure need to complement "soft" capacities that concern management knowledge and skills and well as social expertise and skills such as facilitation, integrity, effective coordination and communication. Soft capacity building has been a focus of **Austria**, where professional associations promote the education and training of water professionals, institutions and stakeholders at large. In **Ireland**, it is the responsibility of the Environmental Protection Agency to provide support and advice to local authorities, through the Network for Ireland's Environmental Compliance and Enforcement (NIECE). This is a complex task as the EPA also has responsibility to supervise the environmental enforcement activities of local authorities (OECD, 2018[1]).

According to the OECD Survey on "Scoping Existing Capacity Development Activities" amongst members of the OECD Water Governance Initiative, most respondents (72%) are already using some parts or the whole set of the Principles on Water Governance as part of ongoing activities related to capacity development, whether governance works as an independent module or integrated in others. However, there is little available information on the long-term impact of capacity development on the improvement of water governance outcomes overall. Moreover, the lack of funding represents a major obstacle for carrying out capacity development on a more consistent basis.

6.5. Use data and information to guide policy

The Recommendation asks Adherents to "produce, update, and share timely, consistent, comparable and policy-relevant water and water-related data and information, and use it to guide, assess and improve water policy."

Improving water governance requires hydrological, technical, social, economic and financial data (i.e. water-related quantifiable and qualitative facts) and information (i.e. interpreted data related to water). Production and access to consistent, comparable and easily accessible information is essential to analyse every situation objectively and devise water strategies to improve policy performance in terms of economic efficiency, equity and environmental sustainability. Many Adherents have set up integrated water information systems and databases as **Spain** (an open access national database includes the information of the 25 RBMP [6]), **Portugal** (National Water Resources Information System [SNIRH]), **Australia** (Water Resources Information System [AWRIS]), and **France** (national system of water information - SISPEA)

(OECD, 2018[1]). The Spanish water sector is going through a digital transformation process to improve the quality of the water-related data and information. It is expected to allow linking new technologies (i.e. IA, deep learning, big data) with advanced operation processes, including production (basin, waste water treatment plant and groundwater), transport and drinking water supply and sewerage networks. The digital transformation process is expected to include all the stakeholders simultaneously: different levels of government officials, the private sector, regulators, service providers, other relevant constituencies and the population who should be able to perceive the final result of that end-to-end data governance model.

Within the reporting and compliance approach of the **European Union** Water Framework Directive, the Water Information System (WISE) provides a web-portal entry to water-related information ranging from inland waters to marine, grouped into the following sections: EU water policies, data and themes, modelling and projects and research. The WISE is based on a partnership between the European Commission (DG Environment, Joint Research Centre and Eurostat) and the European Environment Agency, known as "the Group of Four" (Go4). It was launched for public use in 2007 (OECD, 2015[4]).

Relevant data on water resources and water services is the basis for tailored water governance strategies, measurement of results and indications of possible bottlenecks. Central governments may not find it easy to promote and assess water resources and service strategies without obtaining information from sub-national governments. For example, in **Mexico**, nine states agreed to develop an information system on water quantity (availability and coverage) and quality for the various river basins and sub-basins in their region in 2004 (OECD, 2013[6]).

Production and exchange of information is also vital to building trust and a shared vision among responsible authorities and stakeholders. National statistical offices have a key role in generating such data and/or providing the harmonisation of metrics to allow comparability across units and time. Sub-national levels of government and regional/local development agencies also have an important role to play in collecting and using data to inform the water policy process. In 2013, **Turkey** created an online National Water Information System (NWIS) that compiles nationwide data on water quality and quantity, allocation regimes and water-related risks. The NWIS shows water data at basin level and aims to encourage all water-related actors to be active stakeholders in data production. Furthermore, the NWIS helps identify data gaps and duplications and gather data, maps, statistics and policy documents under nine modules: environmental infrastructure, basin management, climate change, groundwater, surface water, water quality, drought, floods and water allocation (OECD, 2018[1]). **Ireland** has followed a tiered approach to characterisation, which has resulted in structured data and scientific evidence at national, catchment area (46), sub-catchment (583) and water body (4 829) levels. The data are all gathered into one new IT application called the Water Framework Directive (WFD) Application, operated by the Irish Environmental Protection Agency, and all public bodies involved in water management and protection in Ireland have access to it (OECD, 2018[1]). In **Israel**, a new tariff established for industries producing effluents with a high concentration of pollutants has encouraged the development of a high-tech information system for water quality. When the tariff was set in 2011 technologies used for monitoring those effluents improved significantly. The new online measuring systems provide useful information that guides water services management, such as forecast changes in water consumption, quasi-real time leakage detection, etc. As a result, municipal water and sewage corporations have improved the quality of the water services delivered (water leakages have decreased from approximately 30% ten years ago to a national average of less than 11%) (OECD, 2018[1]). This kind of information is crucial for stakeholders to continue improving water service, as well as an effective system for monitoring, early warning, and decision support in the water sector governance, as well as a protection against extreme events.

6.6. Mobilise water finance efficiently

The Recommendation asks Adherents to "ensure that governance arrangements help mobilise water finance and allocate financial resources in an efficient, transparent and timely manner."

Insufficient or unstable revenues in the water sector are an important obstacle to the effective implementation of water policies in Adherents.

Coordination across levels of government is necessary to map, align and catalyse funding needs. For example, national water strategies do not always have specific rules on how to finance water.

A number of country examples provide valuable insights to enhance multi-level governance and planning in response to funding needs. For instance, in **Canada**, under the Water Act agreements, several levels of governments share the financial burden of water-related projects: agreements for specific water programmes provide for the participating governments to contribute funding, information and expertise in agreed ratios. For ongoing activities, such as the water quantity survey agreements with each province, cost-sharing is in accordance with each party's need for the data. For study and planning agreements, it is usual for the federal government to meet half the costs and the provincial government the other half. The planning studies encompass interprovincial, international or other basins where federal interests are important. Implementation of planning recommendations occurs on a federal, provincial and federal-provincial basis. Cost-sharing of the construction of major infrastructure works is generally jointly funded by federal, provincial and municipal local governments (OECD, 2015[4]).

Aligning multi-annual strategic plans to annual budgets and medium-term priorities of governments helps the continuity of water policies even cutting across political cycles. In **Portugal**, the six-year strategic plans guided the implementation of the country's water services public policy and were concomitant with EU funding under the umbrella of the Cohesion Funds and other EU programmes. The plan and its revisions every six years have followed a similar structure to ensure consistency (OECD, 2018[1]).

6.7. Implement and enforce water regulation

The Recommendation asks Adherents to "ensure that sound water management regulatory frameworks are effectively implemented and enforced in pursuit of the public interest."

Comprehensive, coherent and predictable regulatory frameworks founded on effective regulatory policies and institutions are essential for setting the rules, standards and guidelines to achieve water policy outcomes. Sound regulation serves to ensure that economies function efficiently while meeting important social and environmental goals. It also builds public trust in the administration as an effective rule maker.

Adherents have adopted different types of regulatory frameworks to ensure the performance of various regulatory functions in relation to water services. Aside from self-regulation, major regulatory models include (OECD, 2009): regulation by government; regulation by contract, which specifies the regulatory regimes in legal instruments (the French model); independent regulation (Anglo-American model); and the outsourcing of regulatory functions to third parties, which makes use of external contractors to perform activities such as tariff reviews, benchmarking and dispute resolution.

The third model – the establishment of dedicated regulatory bodies for water and sanitation services (WWS) – stands out across Adherents as a response to some of the challenges of regulatory frameworks for water services (Figure 6.6). It has also accompanied the reform of the water industry that many Adherents have undergone over the past two decades, in particular in the trend towards corporatisation of water operators and the consolidation of water service provision (in Adherents such as **Ireland** and **Portugal** for instance). Independent WWS regulators necessarily interact with a broad range of institutions. Across the Adherents and territories surveyed by the OECD in 2014 on *Applying Better Regulation in the*

Water Service Sector, WSS regulators are part of a broader regulatory framework at national or sub-national level. This framework typically involves line ministries (environment or natural resources) in charge of water policies, health department in charge of water quality standards and ministries of environment in charge of effluents. Various public agencies, e.g. environmental protection agencies, also play a role in specific issues of water regulation.

Figure 6.6. Status of water regulatory agencies in selected OECD and non-OECD Adherents

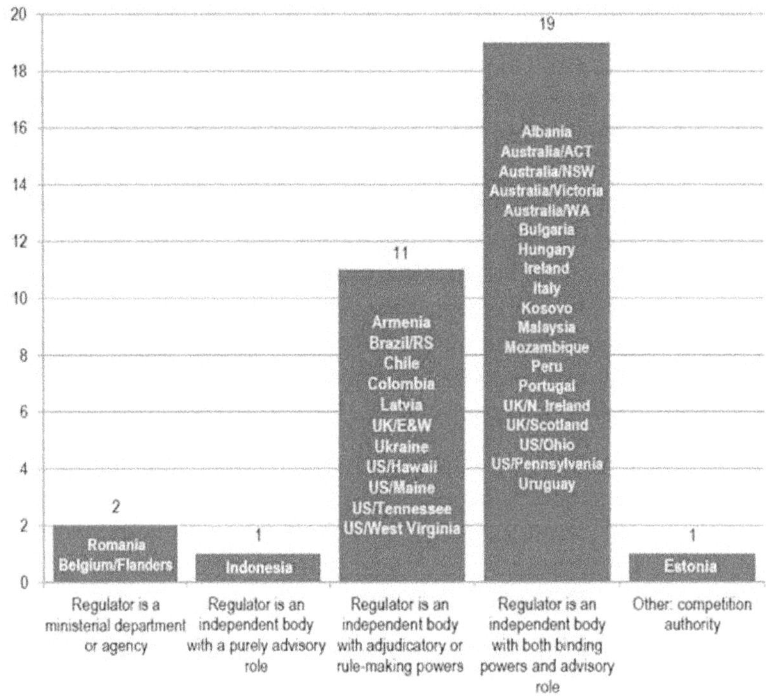

Note: 32 water regulators surveyed

Source: Cited in OECD (2015), The Governance of Water Regulators, OECD Studies on Water, OECD Publishing, Paris, https://doi.org/10.1787/9789264231092-en.

Data from the OECD Indicators on the Governance of Sector Regulators (OECD, 2018)[7] reveal the performance of 16 water regulators in Adherents. The database includes data: **Australia, Belgium, Chile, Czech Republic, Denmark, Estonia, Hungary, Ireland, Israel, Italy, Korea, Latvia, Netherlands, Portugal, Slovak Republic and United Kingdom**. All 16 regulators have their objectives and functions defined in legislation. This contributes to ensuring a predictable legal and institutional framework for the sector. Several regulators undertake measures to ensure that they are transparent as an institution, as are their rules and processes (Table 6.1, rows a-d). This can include by reporting on their activities (all 16 regulators), publishing forward-looking action plans (11 out of 16), publishing all their decisions, resolutions and agreements (15 out of 16) and showing how they have come to decisions by providing evidence and data (14 out of 16). Many regulators also use regulatory tools, such as evaluation and consultation mechanisms, to foster the quality of regulatory processes and make the results accessible to the public (rows e-h). In many cases, it is notable that regulators go beyond their legal requirements in terms of transparency and stakeholder engagement. For example, all the surveyed regulators report on their activities, even if this is not a legislative requirement (**Czech Republic**, **Estonia** and **Great Britain)** (row a). Similarly, providing feedback on the comments received from stakeholders is rarely a legislative requirement, yet in total 13 out of 16 regulators do so, including eight where it is not required by law (**Australia, Belgium, Denmark, Estonia, Ireland, Italy, Netherlands, United Kingdom**).

Table 6.1. Governance Arrangements in Water Regulators

	AUS	BEL	CHL	CZE	DNK	EST	HUN	IRL	ISR	ITA	KOR	LVA	NLD	PRT	SVK	GBR	Key
a. Is there a legislative requirement for the regulator to publish a report on its activities?	●	●	●	♦	●	♦	●	●	●	●	●	●	●	●	●	♦	Yes: ● No, but the regulator produces it: ♦
b. Is the publication of a forward-looking action plan a legislative requirement to enhance the transparency of the regulator's activities?	●	-	-	●	-	●	-	●	●	●	●	●	●	-	●	●	Yes: ● No/not applicable: -
c. Is the publication of all decisions, resolutions and agreements a legislative requirement to enhance the transparency of the regulator's activities?	●	-	●	●	●	●	●	●	●	●	●	●	●	●	●	●	Yes: ● No/not applicable: -
d. Does the regulator need to motivate its regulatory decisions (e.g. with evidence and data)?	●	-	●	♦	-	●	●	●	♦	♦	●	●	●	●	●	●	Yes, all decisions: ● Yes, but not all decisions: ♦ No: -
e. Does the regulator publish draft decisions and collect feedback from stakeholders?	♦	-	-	●	♦	♦	-	♦	●	♦	●	●	●	●	●	♦	Yes, in line with a legislative requirement: ● Yes, even if there is no legislative requirement: ♦ No: -
f. Does the regulator provide feedback on comments received by stakeholders?	♦	♦	-	●	♦	♦	-	♦	-	♦	●	●	♦	●	●	♦	Yes, in line with a legislative requirement: ● Yes, even if there is no legislative requirement: ♦ No: -
g. Is public consultation on relevant activities a legislative requirement?	●	-	●	-	●	●	●	●	●	●	●	●	●	●	●	●	Yes: ● No/not applicable: -
h. Does the regulator collect information on the quality of regulatory process of the regulator?	●	●	●	-	●	●	●	●	●	●	●	●	●	●	-	●	Yes: ● No/not applicable: -

Source: OECD (2018) Database on the Governance of Sector Regulators

6.8. Promote innovative water governance practices

The Recommendation asks Adherents to "promote the adoption and implementation of innovative water governance practices across responsible authorities, levels of government and relevant stakeholders."

Innovation is important in the water sector and can support change towards more sustainable and water secure futures. The extent to which innovations can be effectively implemented and scaled-up is subject to enabling governance frameworks.

In order to implement innovative systems, there is a widely acknowledged need for improved water governance across multiple levels of administration, sectors and stakeholders that can manage water for multiple values. Several Adherents have put in place "pacts" to achieve common goals across levels of governments and build capacities. For example, in the **Netherlands**, the Climate Adaptation City Deal was signed in 2016 between the Ministry of Infrastructure and the Environment, three regional water authorities, five cities (The Hague, Dordrecht, Gouda, Rotterdam and Zwolle) and seven other partners (research centres and companies). The aim was to create a learning environment for climate adaptation at urban level for the next four years. In particular, it promoted innovative ideas to tackle flood risks, to foster an integrated approach between water and spatial planning, and to enhance co-operation in general (Charbit and Romano, 2017[11]). Another example of this type of practice is the contracts between the municipality of Paris (**France**), where authorities in the hinterland and farmers to foster co-operation between supplying areas in terms of water resources and the urban core. The city water operator, Eau de Paris, has been involved in two programmes – Phyt'Eaux Cités and Preri – to preserve and improve water quality in its catchment areas, in partnership with the river basin agency of Seine- Normandie. The first programme, Phyt'Eaux Cités, encourages suburban communities, golf courses, garden centres and transportation networks to reduce or stop their use of pesticides in the Yvette, Orge and Seine basins. The second programme, Preri, aims to prevent industrial risks near the Seine and Yerres rivers by identifying and monitoring potentially dangerous sites in terms of industrial waste (OECD, 2016[5]).

Good practices include promoting innovative ways to co-operate, to pool resources and capacity, to build synergies across sectors and search for efficiency gains. An example is a multi-stakeholder committee (representatives from community organisations, the industrial sector, government departments, other levels of government and municipal services) in Montreal (**Canada**) that helped improve the quality of discharged water in catchment areas. New York City (**United States**) has also created an agreement with watershed communities and other authorities helped to preserve both water quality and the economic dynamism of the area through urban-rural partnerships (OECD, 2016[5]). A kind of co-operation based on the participation of higher levels of government are Consortia (**Italy, Spain**), which are standing organisations with a board and staff for drinking water supply cycle (from production to distribution) (i.e. Greater Bilbao Water Partnership, a consortium of 43 municipalities, provincial government of Biscay, the Autonomous Basque Community and central government). Additionally in **France**, there is the *Conseil communautaire,* an elected body that can act on behalf of the municipalities on specific water issues and the Metropolitan Authority of Barcelona (**Spain**) that has fostered an integrated perspective across local governments as well as shared infrastructure and expenses (OECD, 2016[5]).

The implementation of innovative practices has already occurred in terms of new forms of data and information sharing through collaboration with various stakeholders, like universities and specified government systems. For example, in 2017, **Turkey**, integrated the National Water Information System into Turkey's "E-government" system, an online public portal informing on the quality of public services. The ultimate objective is to promote social learning on water policy and encourage the use of data by non-governmental actors (i.e. academia, NGOs, etc.) (OECD, 2018[1]). In the **Netherlands**, the Waves system is an open data initiative launched by Dutch Water Authorities to promote social learning in the Netherlands. Waves makes large amounts of data on the performance of each water authority available to the public. Every two years, Dutch Water Authorities analyses the data and publishes a report that benchmarks the performance of all the authorities. Besides the open data and the reports, the website also provides tools that allow running simple analyses (OECD, 2018[1]). The **Netherlands** also uses e-participation to set up citizen observatories for flood risk management (OECD, 2015[12]). **Portugal** utilises open data systems in the form of a mobile application developed by the Water and Waste Services Regulation Authority (ERSAR). The app aims to provide relevant information to water and waste services users in Portugal, like the quality of service provided to each user so that users can compare their service to those in other geographical areas. (OECD, 2015[12]).

6.9. Mainstream integrity and transparency

The Recommendation asks Adherents to "mainstream integrity and transparency practices across water policies, water institutions and water governance frameworks for greater accountability and trust in decision-making."

Integrity and transparency are both critical for building and restoring trust in governments and water institutions. Integrity is an indispensable pre-condition to ensure that existing resources and decisions serve society and improve equity, efficiency and sustainability.

Promoting integrity and transparency requires support by the highest authorities and an enabling institutional environment for actors responsible for implementing integrity measures. Therefore, there is a need for integrity and transparency in all water-related policies and institutions, legislation and regulation at various levels, investment projects and programmes, and in business models for public and private entities working in water resources management and water service provision. This has occurred in the International Commission for the Protection of the Danube River, which flows through several EU member states (**Germany, Austria, Czech Republic, Slovak Republic, Hungary, Croatia, Romania and Bulgaria**). It has developed rules of procedure to mainstream integrity and transparency practices to increase accountability and trust in the decision-making process of the commission. These rules range from the fundaments of treaties to organisational rules for staff members of the permanent secretariat. The commission also supports the active involvement of stakeholders and civil society through observer organisations as well as public consultation processes for the development of basin management plans (OECD, 2018[1]).

Following a call for greater transparency and accountability in the water sector, in the **Netherlands** benchmarking has developed in the last decade. Existing benchmarks differ according to number of associated organisations and with respect to ranking, learning and exchange of best practices, and development of key performance indicators. In addition to these benchmarks, the Consumer Association (Consumentenbond) also plays an important role in terms of customer interest protection with regard to all aspects related to water and sanitation, especially the quality of services.

6.10. Promote stakeholder engagement

The Recommendation asks Adherents to "promote stakeholder engagement for informed and outcome-oriented contributions to water policy design and implementation".

The water sector involves a plethora of public, private and not-for-profit stakeholders. In addition to policy makers and governments, citizens, private actors, end users, investment banks, and infrastructure and service providers have a stake in the outcome of water policy and with whom engagement needs therefore to be sought (Box 6.1).

Box 6.2. Stakeholder engagement

Stakeholder engagement refers to the process by which any person or group who have an interest or stake in a water related topic, and/or have the ability to influence the outcome positively or negatively, are involved in the related activities and decision-making processes, as well as how water policy may directly or indirectly affect the actors involved. It implies that all stakeholders, including vulnerable and resource-poor groups, are meaningfully involved in deciding the use, protection, management and allocation of water (OECD, 2015[12]). A distinction is also necessary between public participation and stakeholder engagement. The former encompasses a range of procedures and methods designed to consult, involve and inform local communities and citizens (i.e. the "public", essentially civil society and customers). The latter opens a broader perspective to different groups of actors, including levels of governments, the private sector, regulators, service providers, donor agencies, investors and other relevant constituencies, in addition to civil society in its different forms (e.g. non-governmental organisations, citizen movements, etc.).

There are six levels of stakeholder engagement depending on the processes and the intentions they pursue (Figure 6.7). *Communication* intends to make water-related information and data available to other parties and to raise awareness involving open dialogue with the targeted audience on a specific water-related issue. *Consultation* aims to gather stakeholders' comments, perceptions, information, advice, experiences and ideas. *Participation* insinuates the association of stakeholders within the decision-making process and that they take part in discussions and activities. *Representation* involves the development of a collective choice by aggregating preferences from various stakeholders, often officially representing the perspectives and interests of stakeholders in the management of a project or an organisation. *Partnerships* consist of agreed-upon collaboration between institutions, organisations or citizen to combine resources and competencies in relation to a common project or challenge to solve. *Co-production and co-decisions* are characterised by a balanced share of power over the policy or project decision-making process. They transform the relationship between stakeholders, enabling each of them to take more control and ownership, and contributing to the alignment of policy or project outcomes with their aspirations and needs.

Figure 6.7. Levels of stakeholder engagement

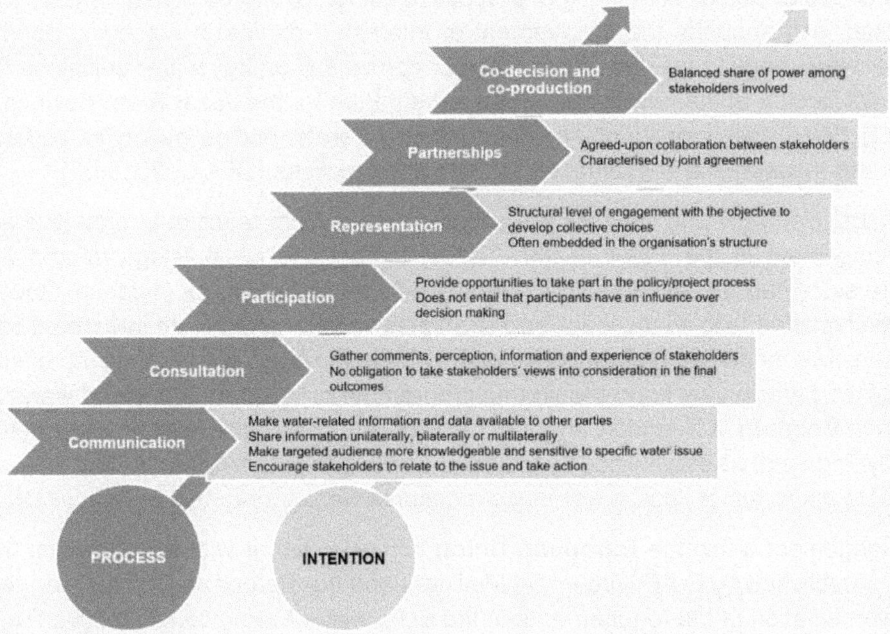

Source: OECD (2015), Stakeholder Engagement for Inclusive Water Governance, OECD Studies on Water, OECD Publishing, Paris. http://dx.doi.org/10.1787/9789264231122-en

Source: The OECD Water Indicator Framework, OECD, 2019. https://www.oecd.org/cfe/regional-policy/oecd-water-governance-indicator-framework.htm

Evaluating the effectiveness of the engagement process and outcomes can shed light on the contribution of stakeholder engagement to better water governance. Conducting evaluations on the costs and benefits of stakeholder engagement can provide the evidence to effectively guide decision making and policy/project implementation with tangible data and analyses. The costs of stakeholder engagement relate to the different phases of the engagement process and concern the production and disclosure of needed information, operational expenses (facilities, travel, staff, overtime, etc.) or opposition to the final decisions, as well as delays in decision making or implementation. Overall, benefits can be clustered into four types: acceptability and sustainability (e.g. effective implementation, proper enforcement of regulation, political acceptability, ownership of decision and outcomes); social equity and cohesion (e.g. trust, confidence, customer satisfaction, corporate social responsibility); capacity development (e.g. awareness raising, information sharing, opinion forming); and economic efficiency (e.g. cost saving, value for money, time saving, broader economic benefits as policy coherence, synergies across projects) (OECD, 2015[12]).

In **Germany**, the National Water Dialogue embraces a multi-governance level approach, engaging all levels of administrations and all relevant stakeholders, even beyond the water sector, as well as citizens, in order to develop a shared vision on water management. The first National Water Forum took place in October 2018 in Berlin to discuss the problems and challenges of water governance and management in Germany. This Forum brought together 130 participants from a variety of sectors. The Ministry of Environment will draft a National Water Strategy by 2021 based on this Dialogue process and according to a number of guiding principles. The National Water Dialogue and ensuing Strategy constitutes the response to the demand from participating stakeholders that water needs to play a greater role in environmental policy and more value needs to be attached to the quality of water within society. The Strategy will thus recognise and enforce the political significance of water as the basis for life and its linkages to other sectors such as agriculture, energy and health (Gruère, Ashley and Cadilhon, 2018[9]).

Spain also has a long history of multi-stakeholder decision making for water resources management, reinforced by the requirements of the WFD. The Júcar river basin authority promotes information, consultation and public participation in the process leading to the establishment of the river basin management plan, and supports the involvement of interested parties in achieving good status of the Mancha Oriental water body to build multi-stakeholder consensus on key water decisions. This led to the adoption by Royal Decree of the new Water Management Plan for the Júcar River Basin in July 2014, as required by the EU WFD, with monitoring and control tools for water bodies' quality and quantity; resource-saving actions; and measures to substitute water pumping practices (OECD, 2015[12]).

A clear set of rules, platforms and vehicles are critical to move from reactive to proactive and systematic stakeholder engagement in the water sector. These platforms exist in **Belgium** and **France**, where stakeholders are systematically engaged in establishing flood-risk maps, for instance. Governments must also establish such platforms to shape long-term strategies and plans within an integrated basin approach. As flood risk intensifies, engaging property developers and landowners will become increasingly important as in the case of the participatory flood-monitoring programme of Vivaqua, a drinking water and sanitation service provider in **Belgium**. It is equally important to ensure that marginalised or vulnerable stakeholders are also properly engaged, as exemplified by the flood prevention programme of Alsace-Moselle (**France**), where the benefits and costs of flood governance measures were distributed equitably (OECD, 2019[2]).

Stakeholder engagement within the **European Union** comes together with the Common Implementation Strategy (CIS), established by EU Environment Ministers and the European Commission, which supports Adherents' implementation of the requirements of the EU's Water Framework Directive. The CIS ensures the full involvement of stakeholders such as water users, public authorities, the scientific community, international organisations and non-governmental organisations (civil society) in the preparation and adoption of policy documents and guidance in support of member Adherents' implementation of the Directive. The CIS ensures that stakeholders an active role in informing the implementation process and in preparing decisions, activities and outputs from the process. It works at three distinct levels: working groups, a Strategic Co-ordination Group (SCG) and a Water Directors' Group. In most cases, issues reach consensus in the working groups and the SCG (OECD, 2015[4]).

In 2008, the Ontario government (**Canada**) passed the Lake Simcoe Protection Act, which established two permanent committees that engage multiple stakeholders in decision-making, the Lake Simcoe Science Committee and the Lake Simcoe Co-ordinating Committee, to guide the ongoing efforts to protect the watershed and the lake. The latter consists of representatives from municipalities, Aboriginal communities, the Lake Simcoe Conservation Authority, the province, agricultural and industrial sectors, interest groups and the public. Through an extensive process of stakeholder engagement, the Lake Simcoe Protection Plan was developed and released in 2009. The process allowed diverse stakeholders to provide input on potential actions, including designated policies within the plan that have legal weight to protect sensitive parts of that watershed (OECD, 2015[4]).

In the **Netherlands**, the Delta Programme involves multiple stakeholders, as it is a joint endeavour between the Ministry of Infrastructure and Environment, provinces, municipal councils and regional water authorities, in close co-operation with social organisations and business. Its two priority goals are to protect the Netherlands against flooding and ensure freshwater supply over the next 100 years. Stakeholder engagement within this programme has led to customisation in the strategies and the commitment of several parties at a regional (within the sub-programmes) and national level. Building on multi-stakeholder dialogue, and technical calculations and assumptions, the Delta Programme is governed by several decisions that instruct what measures should be taken for flood risk management (standards, strategies), freshwater strategy, water levels, protection of the delta and spatial adaptation (OECD, 2015[12]).

6.11. Manage governance complexity and trade-offs

The Recommendation asks Adherents to "encourage water governance frameworks that help manage trade-offs across water users, rural and urban areas, and generations".

In the Fitzroy River basin (**Australia**), an indigenous community from Australia has developed a political declaration aiming to protect the traditional and environmental values that underpin basin's heritage. The aboriginal community has been the traditional guardian of the river for centuries, but increasing development in the watershed is jeopardising the future of the river and its people (OECD, 2018[1]). As a result of the "Fitzroy River Declaration", which has been developed based on the OECD Principles, the Government of Western Australia committed to a catchment management plan for the River as well as designated national park areas in parts of the Fitzroy and Margaret Rivers for greater stakeholder engagement.[8]

In terms of managing trade-offs across water users, rural and urban areas, and between generations, a constructive dialogue is a key component. For example, **Mexico** created the River Basin Commission of the Tecocomulco Lagoon in 2005 as an auxiliary structure of the Mexico Valley River Basin Council with the objective to reverse serious risks of deterioration. It is composed of representatives from different levels of government (federal, state, municipal), water users and civil society organisations. It has responsibilities in land and water conservation, as well as sanitation and training activities to foster integrated water resources management (IWRM) and water conflict resolution in the lagoon. The commission builds on constructive dialogues across sectors that had been historically antagonistic. Regular and dynamic meetings as well as monitoring agreements since its creation have positioned the commission as an instance of trusted social participation. It is taken as a reference by consulting regional governments for the implementation of their development programmes at basin level (OECD, 2015[12]).

6.12. Monitor and evaluate water policy and governance

The Recommendation asks Adherents to "promote regular monitoring and evaluation of water policy and governance where appropriate, share the results with the public and make adjustments when needed."

Evaluation can help determine whether water policies work well and learn from experience to improve practice in the future. For example, **Ireland** conducted a comprehensive review (in 2010 and 2014) to assess to what extent water policy fulfils the intended outcomes. As a result, a new three-tier interlocking governance structure was created with a much stronger focus on collaboration, role clarity, hard science and evidence, integrated catchment management, and public engagement (OECD, 2018[1]). Under the **Australian** Water Act 2007, the Productivity Commission (PC) is required to undertake triennial assessments into the progress in achieving the objectives and outcomes of the National Water Initiative (NWI) (e.g. strong and effective water governance; improved efficiency and productivity of water use; improved sustainability of water management; benefits to regional, rural and urban communities etc.) and the need for any future reform. The first PC assessment, published in 2018, called for Council of Australian Governments to renew the NWI by 2020, which is still pending at the time of writing. Regular evaluations, especially when mandated, can also help reconsider the adequacy of existing policies and thereby facilitating the first steps towards necessary reforms (Gruère and Le Boëdec, 2019[13]).

Data can also inform the effects and effectiveness of implemented or planned measures on the reduction of risk (e.g. the geographical information system, or GIS-Tool of the ICPR in the case of the Rhine transboundary basin). In **Poland**, **Belgium** (Flanders), **France** and **England** for instance, the government is using cost-benefit analyses to increase the efficiency of flood governance approaches (OECD, 2019[2]). This includes political, social, and environmental risks. In **Portugal**'s Water and Waste Services Regulation Authority (ERSAR) created a customised system of performance indicators (16 for drinking water supply services and 16 for urban wastewater management services) to support the implementation of water services policies and assess the quality of service provided. ERSAR assesses results of the indicators for each service provider and benchmarks them against other service providers. The information is publicly available and feeds official national and European statistics, as well as relevant policy discussions and decisions. It guides the elaboration and review of the national strategic plans for water services.

A robust evaluation can also be an effective form of risk management. Monitoring frameworks can also draw on indicators at different levels, such as the EU Floods Directive monitoring system (e.g. the Floods Directive Scoreboard, the EU Court of Justice ruling for non-compliance), national supervision (e.g. flood safety standards) or municipal assessments (e.g. on risks and costs of flood events in land-use planning). This raises questions as to how monitoring and evaluation results can link back into the flood management process in an iterative manner and at appropriate intervals delays and formats. For example, **France** approved local strategies and action programmes on territories exposed to floods in 2016, in accordance with their related Flood Risk Management Plans. However, these monitoring and approval processes can at times be hampered by time mismatches, and some local strategies cannot be included in Flood Risk Management Plans because they cannot be finalised by the time these plans are to be issued (OECD, 2019[2]).

References

Charbit, C. and O. Romano (2017), "Governing together: An international review of contracts across levels of government for regional development", *OECD Regional Development Working Papers*, No. 2017/04, OECD Publishing, Paris, https://dx.doi.org/10.1787/ff7c8ac4-en. [11]

Gruère, G., C. Ashley and J. Cadilhon (2018), "Reforming water policies in agriculture: Lessons from past reforms", *OECD Food, Agriculture and Fisheries Papers*, No. 113, OECD Publishing, Paris, https://dx.doi.org/10.1787/1826beee-en. [9]

Gruère, G. and H. Le Boëdec (2019), "Navigating pathways to reform water policies in agriculture", *OECD Food, Agriculture and Fisheries Papers*, No. 128, OECD Publishing, Paris, https://dx.doi.org/10.1787/906cea2b-en. [13]

OECD (2019), *Applying the OECD Principles on Water Governance to Floods: A Checklist for Action*, OECD Studies on Water, OECD Publishing, Paris, https://dx.doi.org/10.1787/d5098392-en. [2]

OECD (2019), *Water Governance in Argentina*, OECD Studies on Water, OECD Publishing, Paris, https://dx.doi.org/10.1787/bc9ccbf6-en. [10]

OECD (2018), *Implementing the OECD Principles on Water Governance: Indicator Framework and Evolving Practices*, OECD Studies on Water, OECD Publishing, Paris, https://dx.doi.org/10.1787/9789264292659-en. [1]

OECD (2016), *Water Governance in Cities*, OECD Studies on Water, OECD Publishing, Paris, https://dx.doi.org/10.1787/9789264251090-en. [5]

OECD (2015), *Drying Wells, Rising Stakes: Towards Sustainable Agricultural Groundwater Use*, OECD Studies on Water, OECD Publishing, Paris, https://dx.doi.org/10.1787/9789264238701-en. [7]

OECD (2015), *Stakeholder Engagement for Inclusive Water Governance*, OECD Studies on Water, OECD Publishing, Paris, https://dx.doi.org/10.1787/9789264231122-en. [12]

OECD (2015), *Water Resources Governance in Brazil*, OECD Studies on Water, OECD Publishing, Paris, https://dx.doi.org/10.1787/9789264238121-en. [4]

OECD (2014), *Water Governance in the Netherlands: Fit for the Future?*, OECD Studies on Water, OECD Publishing, Paris, https://dx.doi.org/10.1787/9789264102637-en. [3]

OECD (2013), *Making Water Reform Happen in Mexico*, OECD Studies on Water, OECD Publishing, Paris, https://dx.doi.org/10.1787/9789264187894-en. [6]

Republic of Korea (2020), *Article 21 of the "Framework Act of Water Management". 26 May 2020 (partial amendment)*, Ministry of Government Legislation of the Republic of Korea. [8]

Notes

[1] www.oecd.org/governance/oecd-principles-on-water-governance.htm

[2] 2019 OECD Survey on water and agriculture policy changes.

[3] Acapulco de Juarez, Amsterdam, Athens, Barcelona, Belo Horizonte, Bologna, Budapest, Calgary, Chihuahua, Cologne, Copenhagen, Culiacan, Daegu, Edinburgh, Glasgow, Grenoble, Hermosillo, Hong Kong, China; Kitakyushu, Krakow, Lisbon, Liverpool, Malaga, Marseille, Mexico City, Milano, Montreal, Nantes, Naples, New York City, Okayama, Oslo, Paris, Phoenix, Prague, Queretaro, Rio de Janeiro, Rome, San Luis Potosi, Singapore, Stockholm, Suzhou, Toluca, Turin, Tuxtla, Veracruz, Zaragoza and Zibo.

[4] The water basins of the overseas departments of Guadeloupe, Guyana, Martinique and Reunion have a Water Office, with equivalent missions.

[5] 2019 OECD Survey on water and agriculture policy changes.

[6] https://servicio.mapama.gob.es/pphh-web/

[7] The Indicators on the Governance of Sector Regulators (OECD, 2018) capture the governance arrangements of economic regulators in the energy, e-communications, rail transport, air transport and water sectors.

[8] http://www.oecd.org/cfe/regional-policy/Water-Practice-41-OECD-Principles-Fitzroy-River-Australia.pdf

7. Ensuring sustainable finance, investment and pricing for water and water services

This chapter presents Adherents' experience with ensuring sustainable finance, investment and pricing for water resources management and water services, in line with the OECD Recommendation on Water. The chapter describes the principles for financing water resources management. It explores how Adherents aim for the greatest social returns to investments by exploring options that can minimise financing needs, taking stock of existing assets, developing strategic financial plans and setting up independent reviews. Finally, the chapter focuses on diversifying revenue streams and tapping into new sources of capital.

The Recommendation calls on Adherents to "set up measures for the sustainable financing of water services, water infrastructures, water resources management and protection of water-related ecosystems". The 2019 OECD Implementation Water Survey reveals that 63% of respondents (Figure 7.1) have developed a funding strategy alongside their water management plans.

Figure 7.1. Funding strategies for water management plans

Note: Response to question: "Does the water management plan include a dedicated funding strategy to cover costs of its implementation?". For clarification purposes: in Spain, the programme of measures details economic information for each measure, including the way in which it will be financed, which competent authority will be responsible of both the financing and the implementation, financial and other type of costs, planning and financial projections over the years. Canada and the USA do not have national water management plans: water planning efforts occur at both state and sub-state levels.
Source: 2019 survey on the implementation of the OECD Council Recommendation on Water; 27 responses received, including 26 Adherents.

Country-level projections provide estimates of the level of financing needed to meet future water infrastructure and service demands. Financing needs are driven by factors such as urban population growth, the need to adapt to climate change, or changes in the appropriate levels of water security (which translates into more stringent regulations). For example, in Europe, investment needs in all EU member states are projected to increase by more than 25% by 2030, to comply with the Drinking Water Directive and Urban Wastewater Treatment Directives (Figure 7.2) (OECD, 2020[1]).

Figure 7.2. Distance to compliance with the EU Directives on Drinking Water and Urban Wastewater Treatment

Annual additional expenditures required, as a share of current level of expenditure

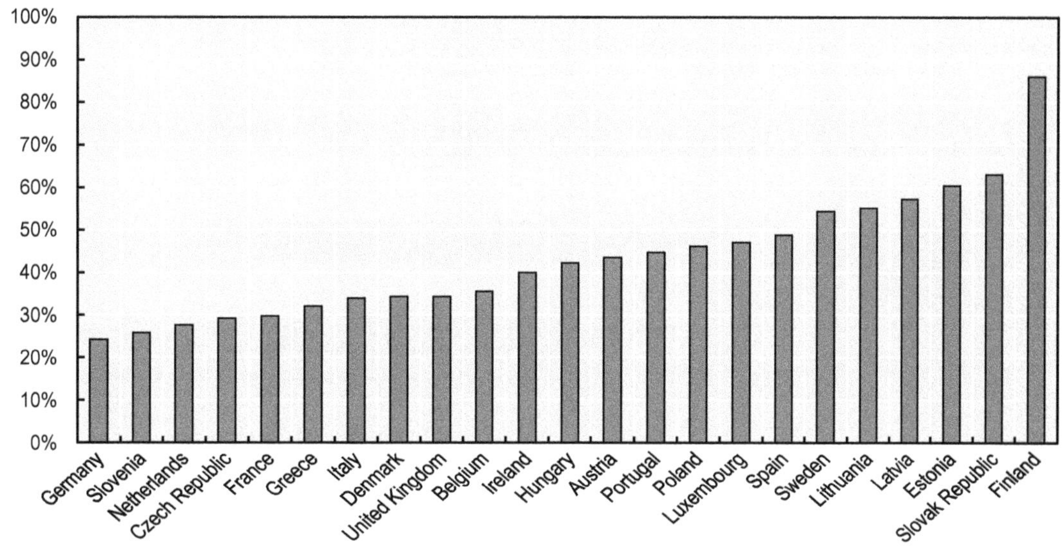

Source: (OECD, 2020[1])

Issues related to the sustainability of financing strategies for water-related infrastructure are not limited to water supply and sanitations services. As regards agriculture water, renewal of existing assets require additional expenditure. For instance, **Japan** has invested heavily in its irrigation infrastructure over the last 50 years, but more than 20% of the core irrigation facilities have now exceeded their expected lifespan (OECD, 2019[2]). In light of these challenges, the Recommendation suggests Adherents consider a set of principles for financing water-related infrastructure and water resources management, while aiming for the greatest social returns to investment and diversifying revenue streams.

7.1. Principles for financing water resources management

Adherents to the Recommendation should "Consider four principles for financing water resources management: Polluter Pays, Beneficiary Pays, Equity and Coherence between policies that affect water resources." These principles can usefully guide policy decisions for financing water management, notably when designing instruments, and help guide the allocation of scarce public resources (OECD, 2012[3]).Figure 7.3 shows that nearly all Adherents responding to the survey have adopted the Polluter Pays Principle and 17 out of 26 Adherents the Beneficiary Pays Principle. Considerably less, namely only 9 and 10 out of 26 responding Adherents state that equity and policy coherence principles were considered in the context of financing of their water resources management. More detailed reviews would help understand if and how the Principles are taken into account, and implemented on the ground.

Figure 7.3. Consideration of principles for financing water resources management

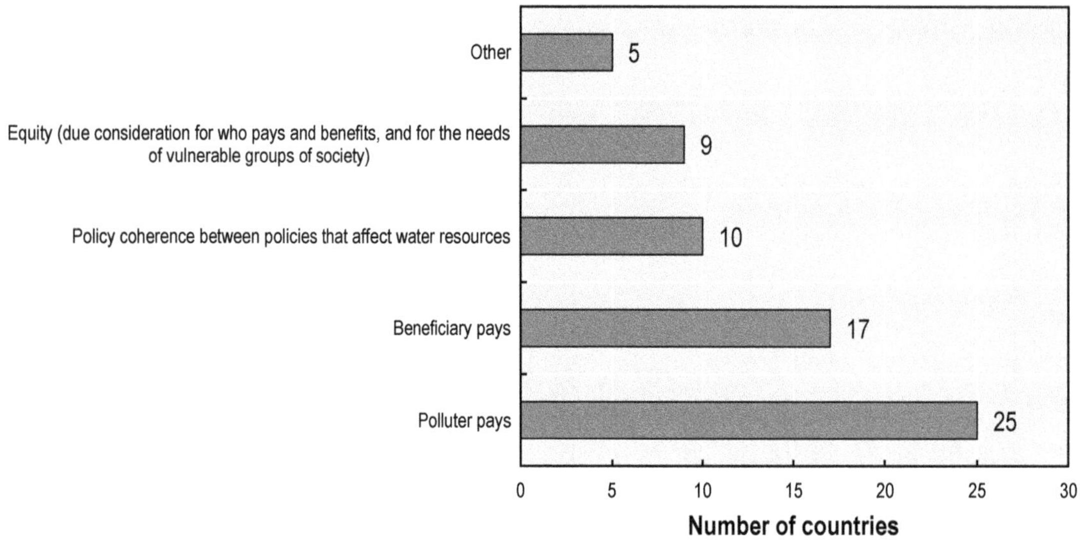

Note: Responses to the question: "Are the following principles for financing water resources management considered in water management planning?". Multiple responses were possible.
Source: 2019 survey on the implementation of the OECD Council Recommendation on Water; 27 responses received, including 26 Adherents.

The *Polluter Pays principle* is considered by over 90% of respondents, based on the 2019 OECD Implementation Survey. It serves the following purposes: either influence behaviour to reduce pollution, or generate revenues to alleviate pollution and compensate for social costs. Framework legislations, such as the **EU** Water Framework Directive (WFD) or the **EU** Waste Water Framework Directive have further encouraged Adherents part of the European Union to embrace this principle (Box 7.1). This principle is reflected in economic instruments, such as taxes and charges (e.g. abstraction or pollution charges) that many Adherents have put in place (see below or further details). Some Adherents, such as **Belgium, Canada, France** or **Spain**, also require industry to pay for managing water pollution, through extended producer responsibility schemes (OECD, 2019[4]). Such schemes transfer some of the costs of treatment to the polluters, and are therefore in alignment with the Polluter Pays Principle. They provide a financial incentive for polluters to invest in less polluting production processes or more sustainable substances/products (Box 7.2).

There are different approaches to the use of revenue of such policy instruments. In **Mexico** for instance, the resources collected in line with this principle are integrated into the general budget for its allocation according to national priorities and not earmarked for water expenditures, thus contributing to higher efficiency of budgetary expenditures.

Box 7.1. Strengthening the application of the polluter pays principle in the European Union

Article 9 of the Water Framework Directive (WFD) requires member states to integrate the Polluter Pays Principle. Countries have to produce an analysis at the scale of each watershed in order to back water pricing policies which encourage users to use resources efficiently and which contributes to the achievement of the WFD good water quality objectives. The fees collected by agencies and water boards are intended to meet this obligation and allow them to finance various actions to preserve and restore aquatic environments. In addition, by sending a price signal to water users, they encourage them to use resources more efficiently and to take better account of their impact on the state of water as well as on other uses of water. Impacts on the ground will vary according to the elasticity of water use to prices, which depends on such features as the degree of water scarcity, awareness of water charges, preferences for water uses.

Source: (OECD, 2020[1]), country contribution

Box 7.2. Recovering costs of advanced wastewater treatment plant upgrades, Germany

The cost of upgrading wastewater treatment plants serving a population of over 5000 persons in Germany with an advanced (fourth) level of treatment has been estimated at EUR 1.2 billion per year or EUR 15.20 per person per year. This would result in a wastewater service tariff increase of, on average, 14-17%, and come at a total cost of EUR 36 billion over 30 years.

One financing option proposed is an extended producer responsibility (EPR) scheme. Under a proposed EPR scheme by the association of German Water Suppliers, pharmaceutical manufacturing companies operating in a river basin would be obliged to contribute to the cost of wastewater treatment according to their share of pollution. The EPR scheme is proposed to operate as follows:

- Establishment of a national water fund and coordination unit to manage the scheme
- Wastewater utilities install advanced (fourth) treatment stage at wastewater treatment plants under specific conditions
- The capital and O&M costs of a wastewater treatment plant upgrade are reported to the national water fund coordination unit
- Each polluting company is obliged to pay for their share of the cost of the upgrade. The share reflects the units of pollution emitted each year, determined by a pollution coefficient (indicator of the environmental harm of the polluting substance) and the volume of pollution emitted each year.
- Funds received from polluting companies in the EPR scheme will be distributed to wastewater utilities to refund the cost of advanced treatment.

Source: Civity (2018), Costs of a fourth treatment stage in wastewater treatment plants and financing based on the polluter pays principle (in German), Civity Management Consultants, Berlin, https://www.bdew.de/media/documents/PI_20181022_Kosten-verursachungsgerechte-Finanzierung-4-Reinigungsstufe-_Klaeranlagen.pdf; personal communication (2019).

The *Beneficiary Pays* principle aims at sharing the costs of water management between different water users such as industry, households and agriculture. The use of payment for ecosystem services illustrates this principle well, whereby beneficiaries pay directly (or indirectly) for the service providers. The city of Paris (**France**), or Munich (**Germany**) run voluntary payment schemes to encourage local farmers to adopt more sustainable organic farming practices, hence paying for improving water quality upstream (OECD, 2015[5]). In the **United Kingdom**, the water regulating agency has encouraged water companies to adopt catchment approaches in which they support improved agriculture practices in upstream farms to reduce downstream pollution (Gruère, Ashley and Cadilhon, 2018[6]). An empirical challenge is to identify beneficiaries (e.g. property developers or tourism industry managing recreational areas) to further implement the Principle and diversify revenue streams. Ultimately, authorities define the appropriate policy instruments (e.g. a tax on land use or property value) to harness identified beneficiaries.

The *Equity* principle focuses on who, within a group of users, bares the costs and benefits of water management. It aims to ensure equity in the access to water services and protection against water-related risks. It is considered in water management only in a limited number of Adherents, including **Costa Rica, Korea**, or **Lithuania** (OECD survey, 2019). When risks are disproportionate for some users, some countries promote solidarity across users. In the **Netherlands,** despite regional disparities regarding water-related risks (e.g. floods, sea-level rise) and regardless of the level of risk exposure, every Dutch citizen takes on a share of the burden by paying taxes to manage these water-related risks (OECD, 2014[7]). The same principle lies behind the **French** Natural Catastrophe (CatNat) compensation scheme, which levies a flat-rate premium on all household and car insurance contracts, independent of their exposure to natural hazards; the revenue is used to pay for damages incurred by disasters as well as to invest in public risk reduction measures (OECD, 2018[8]). While this scheme strongly enforces solidarity, the flat rate contributions have reduced incentives for at-risk communities and households to reduce their exposure and vulnerability to flood risks.

The *Policy Coherence* principle seeks to ensure that different policy areas (agriculture, energy, land use, urban development or trade) do not have negative impacts on water availability, quality and freshwater ecosystems, or increase the cost of water management. At the institutional level, this can be supported by merging responsibilities of water quantity and quality management under one ministry, as did **Korea** in June 2018 (OECD, 2018[9]). It can also be accomplished by combining units focusing on related but different water policies within ministries; in **Denmark**'s Ministry of the Environment and Food, officers working on payment schemes for farmers under the Common Agriculture Policy work on a daily basis with those in charge of regulating water pollution. Only a limited number of Adherents have reported to use this principle in water management planning, including **Chile, Israel** and **Portugal** (OECD, 2019[10]).

Although Adherents often consider these principles for policy-making, the extent to which they are implemented in financing strategies and instruments varies in practice (OECD, 2019[10]). Often, Adherents face difficulties in identifying and targeting polluters, in determining reliable estimates of pollution costs and in enforcing existing regulations. They also face strong political opposition to adequately reflect the policy coherence and polluter pays principles (OECD, 2017[11]). In particular, most OECD governments still employ agriculture support policies that can encourage water pollution (Henderson and Lankoski, 2019[12]), and they do not apply the polluter pays principle consistently in this sector (Gruère and Le Boëdec, 2019[13]) (OECD, 2012[14]).

7.2. Aiming for the greatest social returns to investment

To ensure sustainable water financing, the Recommendation calls on Adherents to "*aim for the greatest social returns to investment*".

There is a compelling case for strengthening the financial sustainability of water services, water infrastructures, water resources management and protection of water-related ecosystems to ensure they bring wider social, economic and environmental benefits. However, this can be challenging in a context where Adherents are concerned by the lack of finance and under pressure from constant and growing need to modernise their infrastructure and address environmental concerns and regulatory obligations (OECD, 2009[15]) (OECD, 2012[16]).

7.2.1. *Explore options that can minimise financing needs*

To maximise the social returns on investments, Adherents should explore "options that can minimise current or future financing needs while addressing trade-offs and exploiting synergies between policy objectives and between short and long term challenges." This helps governments, development finance institutions and other stakeholders take informed decisions (OECD, 2018[17]).

Investment decisions are best supported by robust data, methodologies and analytical tools. Cost-benefit analyses are an effective tool to assess how to minimise financing needs and evaluate trade-offs in water investment decisions at project level. Other tools and methods can be more appropriate to explore synergies from interrelated projects at basin scale, and their impact on water resources (OECD, 2018[17]). The city of Auckland (**New Zealand**) uses innovative data sources and methods for advanced asset management. It uses Geographic Information System (GIS) to overlay actions and investments with a direct or indirect effect on freshwater quality (including storm water asset maintenance, renewal and development; cycleway and road construction; network infrastructure development). This helped find synergies between different policy objectives (OECD, 2015[5]).

Another way to minimise financing needs while exploiting synergies between policy objectives is through the use of ecosystem-based approaches (or nature-based solutions, NBS) to manage water quantity or quality (e.g. treatment of contaminated urban runoff). Under specific conditions, and when implementation challenges are overcome, they can provide such co-benefits as opportunities for improved ecosystem services and biodiversity; reducing ambient air pollution; and mitigation of urban heat island effects (OECD, 2020[18]). Investment in these approaches is also generally less capital intensive, has lower operation, maintenance and replacement costs, avoids lock-in associated with capital intensive grey infrastructure, and appreciates in value over time with the regeneration of nature and its associated ecosystem services (OECD, 2020[11]).

The 2019 Survey of the OECD on the Implementation of the Council Recommendation on Water revealed that 90% of Adherents have included ecosystem-based approaches in their national water management plan. They are applied almost equally across the areas of flood risk, water quantity and water quality management (Figure 7.4).

Figure 7.4. Domains using ecosystem-based approaches

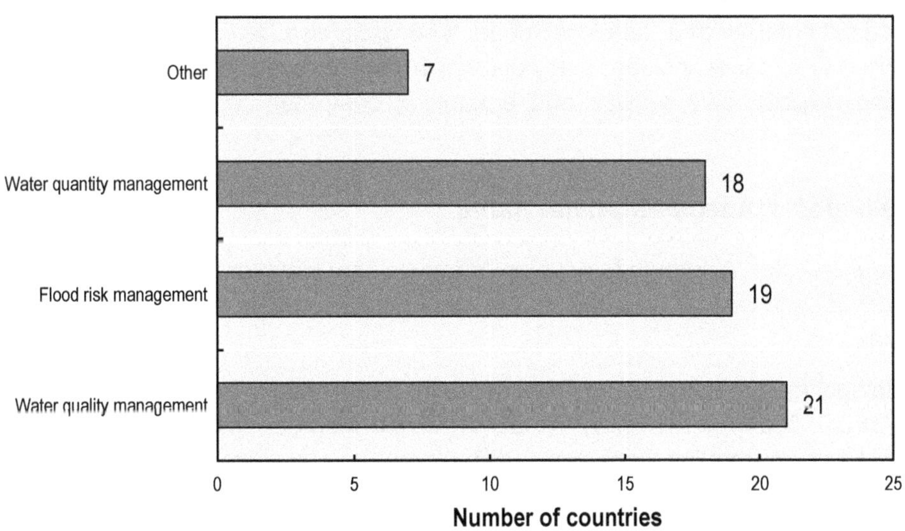

Note: Responses to the question: "In which domains is the use of ecosystem-based approaches suggested?". Multiple responses were possible.

Source: 2019 survey on the implementation of the OECD Council Recommendation on Water; 27 responses received, including 26 Adherents.

The environmental and economic value of employing ecosystem-based approaches has been demonstrated in some key interventions of Adherents. In **Australia**, for example, a pilot project found that rather than upgrading a sewage treatment plant, repairing eroded riparian corridors close to it could achieve the same level of environmental performance at a lower cost (OECD, 2015[5]). In Philadelphia (**United States**), nature-based solutions are used to manage urban floods from heavy rains. These storm water enhancements, managing combined sewer overflows, are bringing about USD 2.6 billion of added benefits and cost less than a conventional upgrade of the current system of pipes and basins (OECD, 2015[5]).

7.2.2. Take stock of existing assets

To further enhance the social returns of water investments, the Recommendation states Adherents should "take stock of existing assets, to maintain them and to look for efficiency gains". Better knowledge of the state of the assets for water supply and sanitation services supports more accurate planning and decisions for operation, maintenance and renewal.

In **France**, the National Observatory of Water and Sanitation Services estimated that close to 160 years would be needed to fully replace the water supply networks and 140 years for replacing the wastewater collection and treatment network at the current pace of renewal. This average hides urban-rural disparities with high-density areas having a significantly faster renewal rate (OECD, 2012[16]). France has required local authorities to do an inventory of public networks for water supply and sanitation; however compliance with this requirement is still low (OECD, 2020[1]). The Japanese Ministry of Health, Labour and Welfare estimated in 2012 that the replacement cost of water supply facilities in 2009 would be about approximately USD 14 billion per year to 2050 to meet the need to renew ageing water infrastructure (most of which in the next 20 years) and to strengthen infrastructure to meet earthquake standards in **Japan** (OECD, 2012[16]). In **Portugal**, the regulator for water and waste services ERSAR has developed and is pilot-testing a set of indicators on infrastructure value and infrastructure management (OECD, 2020[1]).

Artificial Intelligence (AI) technologies have been also used in water utilities to enable a more strategic and cost-effective operation, including better planning and execution of projects and infrastructure, better monitoring and understanding of resource-loss in real time, more efficient collection and distribution networks, and maximum revenue capture and customer satisfaction. These improvements have considerably reduced energy costs, chemical inputs, and water use, as well as enabled better allocation of staff time. Other AI services include chat bots which can be used to answer customer inquiries on demand, ensuring reliable, 24/7 service and enhancing customer satisfaction (OECD, FAO, IIASA, 2020[19]).

7.2.3. Develop strategic financial plans

The Recommendation asks Adherents to develop "strategic financial plans that match financial resources with policy objectives, and ensure affordability for vulnerable segments of society, including through ad hoc targeted measures".

Already a decade ago, most Adherents practiced some form of strategic financial planning for water supply and sanitation (OECD, 2009[15]). Driven by the EU WFD, **EU** member states are required to submit such plans to attract EU funding from the Cohesion and Regional Development budgets. The **Czech Republic**, for example, requires owners of water supply and sewerage systems to draw up and implement financial plans for the replacement of their infrastructure networks. The **United Kingdom** developed a high level strategy and framework for the long term planning of water resources for Public Water Supply in England and Wales. The strategy and framework are updated every five years with the aim of ensuring that there is enough supply of water to meet the anticipated demands of its customers of different water companies, over a minimum 25-year planning period, even under dry conditions.[1]

Ad hoc measures for ensuring the affordability for vulnerable segments of society are taken by a number of Adherents (see below for further details).

7.2.4. Setting up an Independent review

As a final recommendation to maximise social returns to investments Adherents should set up "an independent review of efficiency and cost-effectiveness of investments".

Independent reviews can be undertaken by an independent regulator or a designed authority to ensure that investment decisions, that can have wide ranging impacts, are as efficient and cost-effective. **Australia's** Water Act establishes the independent Murray-Darling Basin Authority to ensure sustainable management of water resources in the country's largest basin and gives the Productivity Commission responsibility for assessing the effectiveness of Basin Plan implementation every five years (OECD, 2019[20]). In **England and Wales** (UK), the Water Services Regulation Authority (OFWAT) reviews company plans on a five-year cycle, using incentive-based regulation to encourage efficiencies and drive down costs. In Scotland (**UK**), the Water Industry Commission for Scotland (WICS) assesses the water-related investment plan every six years with a rolling review every three years to ensure that Scottish Water has visibility for future improvements while having enough flexibility to make the most pressing improvements according to priorities. Similarly in **Portugal**, the Water and Waste Services Regulation Authority (ERSAR) evaluates investments of the state-owned bulk water operators in the beginning of each new regulatory period (OECD, 2015[21]).

7.3. Diversifying revenue streams and tapping into new sources of capital

One final recommendation regarding the sustainable financing of water, proposes that Adherents diversify revenue streams and tap into new sources of capital in line with policy objectives. As a first step it is recommended "to combine revenues from water tariffs, transfers from public budgets and transfers from the international community (i.e. the 3Ts) to recover the costs of investment, operation and maintenance of water infrastructure as much as possible and where efficient".

Adherents use a combination of different financing sources to fund water management (Figure 7.5), most frequently these sources are government budget allocations and revenues from water supply and sanitation tariffs.

Figure 7.5. Adherents' sources of financing for water management

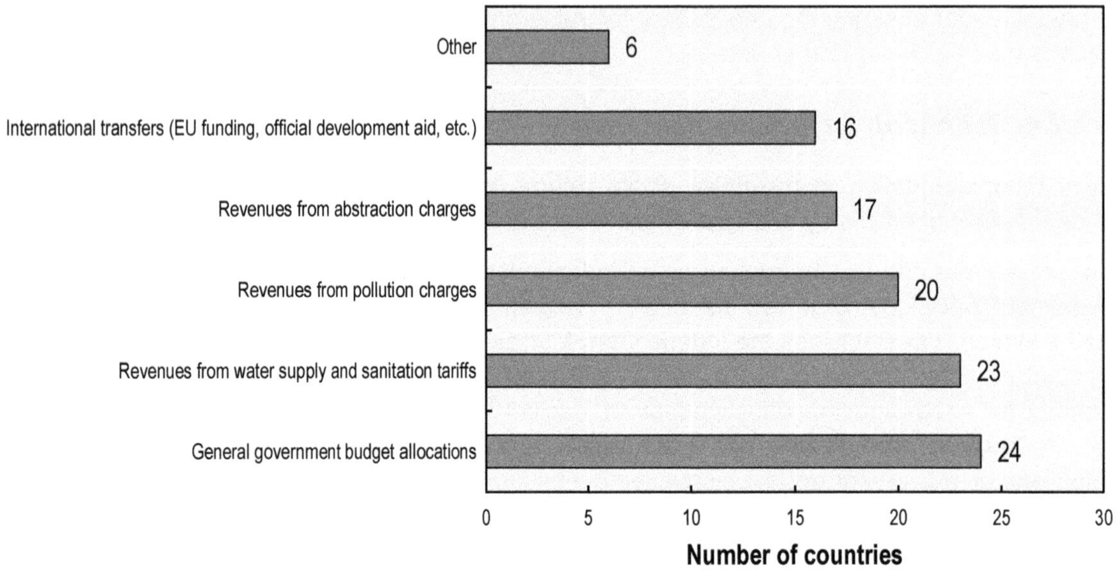

Note: Responses to the question: "What type of sources of financing are used to fund water management?". Multiple responses were possible.
Source: 2019 survey on the implementation of the OECD Council Recommendation on Water; 27 responses received, including 26 Adherents.

In the EU member states revenues from water tariffs and public budgets are shared quite differently, as Figure 7.6 shows. In some Adherents such as **Denmark** tariffs dominate the combined total funding of these two sources, whereas in other Adherents such as the **Netherlands** and **France** they take up a much lower share.

Figure 7.6. Public budgets and household water tariffs as sources of funding for water management

Share of public budgets versus household water tariffs, 2011-15 annual average

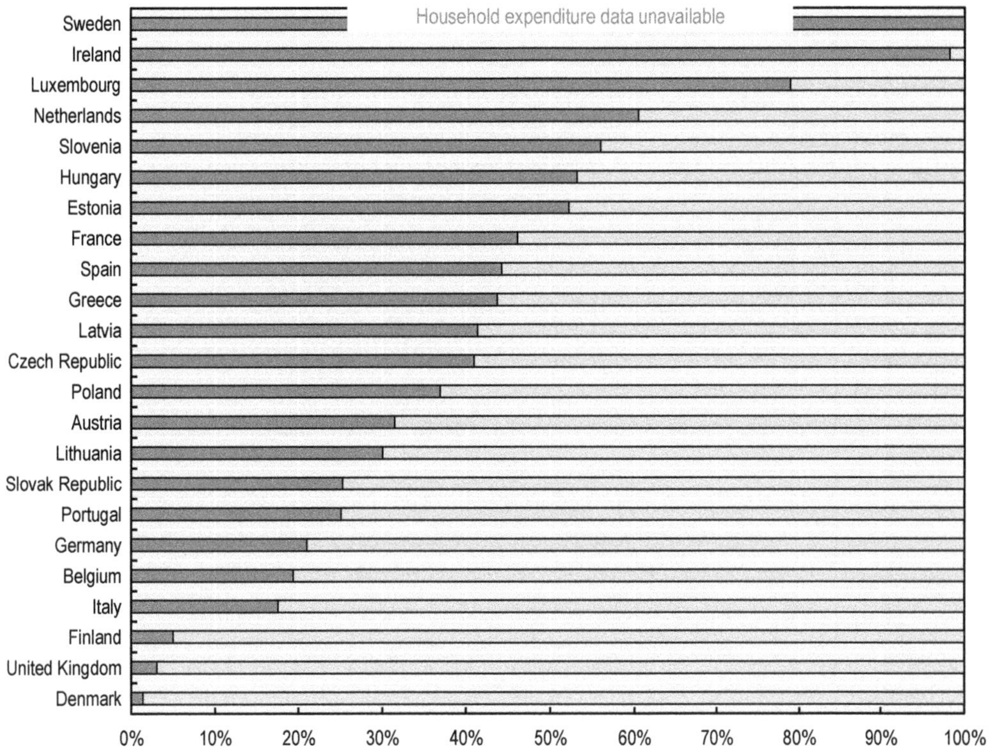

Note: Household expenditures missing for Sweden.
Source: (OECD, 2020[1]); based on EUROSTAT (General government expenditure by function, Final consumption expenditure on environmental protection services by institutional sector, Final consumption expenditure of households by consumption purpose, Mean consumption expenditure by detailed COICOP level).

Some Adherents, such as **Denmark**, rely almost exclusively on tariffs to finance water supply and sanitation-related upfront capital expenditures and operational expenses. Others, such as **Finland, Italy and France** rely on a combination of public and private sources of finance, with an emphasis on household expenditures to cover water supply and sanitation costs. In contrast to that, **Ireland** relies almost exclusively on public expenditures to cover water supply and sanitation-related expenditures. In **Estonia**, **Slovenia** and **Greece** the sources of funding are more evenly distributed between public and household (OECD, 2020[1]).

In addition to general budget transfers, several governments are also levying taxes on actors who benefit from increased water security (including land and property developers) or who generate higher costs and externalities (e.g. owners of large impervious surfaces, such as roads or car parks) (OECD, 2015[5]). Pollution and abstraction charges or taxes exist in a number of Adherents to recover costs and to internalise negative externalities (see chapter 8). The proceeds from these taxes are usually earmarked for water-related expenditures.

In Europe, transfers from the EU is an important source of financing for several member states' investments in water supply and sanitation (Figure 7.7). They account for an average of 13% of total water supply and sanitation expenditures across EU member states. Baltic States (**Estonia, Latvia, Lithuania**) and **Greece** particularly relied on such sources of transfer.

Figure 7.7. Share of EU funding in estimated total expenditures for water supply and sanitation

Percentage, 2011-2015 annual average

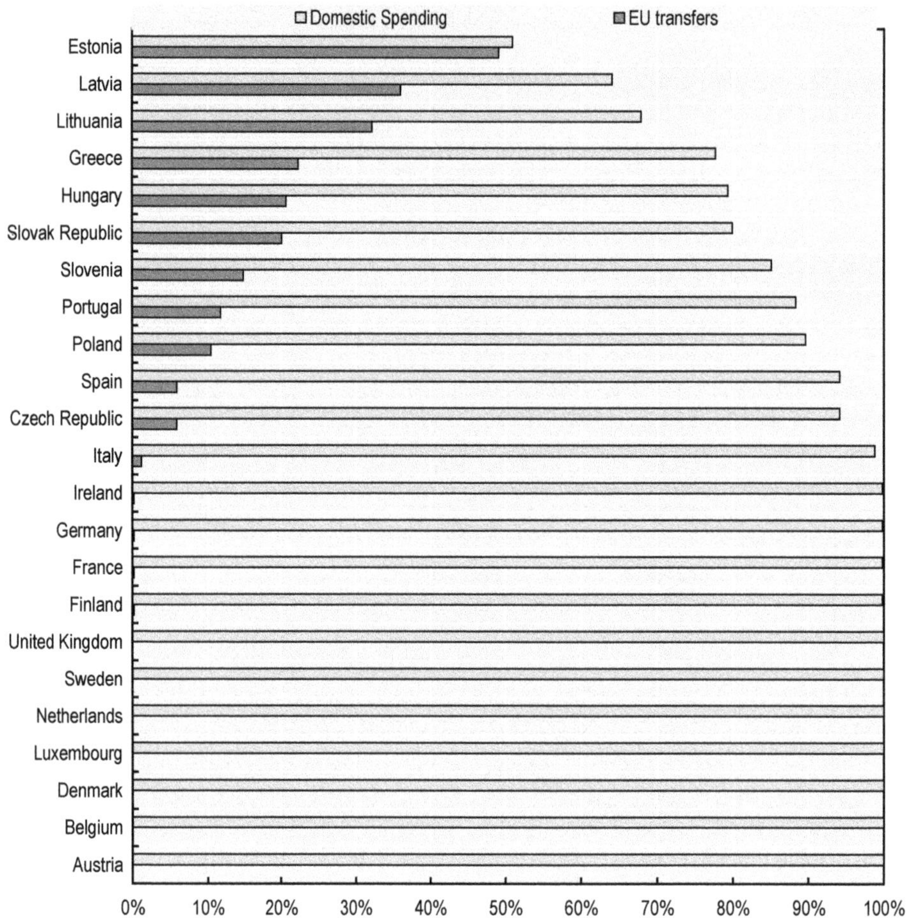

Note: It is assumed that EU funding are always channelled through domestic budgets of each member states and that they are, therefore not additional to government expenditures presented in previous figures.
Source: (OECD, 2020[1]); based on EUROSTAT (for past estimated expenditures), European Commission Directorate-General for Regional and Urban Policy (Open Data Portal for European Structural and Investment Funds).

Outside Europe, international transfers take the form of development assistance. While such transfers are less important in most Adherents, they still account for a significant share of water management funding in some Adherents. In **Cabo Verde**, for example, official development aid pays for 85% of its water production. Japan is one of the donors that has provided development funding for strengthening the country's water supply systems and desalination plants (OECD, 2019[22]).

To bridge any remaining financial gaps for water investments, the recommendation encourages Adherents to consider "tapping into new sources of capital, where needed and in line with policy objectives". Commercial sources of finance (loans, bonds, equity) are used, particularly for covering water supply and sanitation capital expenses, and are repaid from any combination of the 3Ts mentioned above.

Blended finance can play a critical role in mobilising commercial finance and strengthening the financing systems upon which water–related investments rely. The OECD defines blended finance as the strategic use of development finance for the mobilisation of additional finance towards sustainable development in developing countries. Its related principle and range of instruments are relevant for advanced and emerging economies as well (OECD, 2019[22]). Blended finance can add value by shifting funds that are currently not directed to sustainable development in developing countries and sectors that have significant investment needs in order to deliver on the Sustainable Development Goals (SDGs). A recent review of experience with blended finance for water-related investments indicates that blended finance models are emerging but have not reached scale. The success of blended finance is dependent on the ability to mobilise local commercial investment: blended finance for water-related investments reinforces the need for, and benefits from, tailoring blended finance to the local context. In general, blended finance should aim to build local capital markets by working with and mobilising local financiers, as highlighted in the OECD DAC Blended Finance Principles (OECD, 2019[22]).

To effectively tailor blended finance models for water-related investments, an understanding of the underlying business models and value chains is needed. Blended finance models can enter the sector at different points, for example at the water provision or treatment level, downstream at the end-user level or at the investor level. Effective blended finance approaches take into account the business models and respective revenue streams, and incorporate different stakeholder perspectives (OECD, 2019[22]).

Similar reasoning applies to the use of public funding and risk-management instruments to mobilise commercial finance in advance and emerging economies. Notably this applies to the cohesion policy in the European Union, or of public finance more generally. The **United States** has significant experience with water financing models, including State Revolving Funds and more recently, a loan facility to mobilise finance for large-scale water infrastructure established by the Water Infrastructure Financing and Innovation Act (the WIFIA loan programme). **France** uses co-financing mechanisms for drinking water and sanitation services as well as flood protection infrastructure and nature-based solutions: domestic financial institutions such as *Caisse des Dépôts et Consignations* partner with local authorities and water agencies. Note that fiscal regulations in some countries (e.g. **Mexico**) do not allow such arrangements.

References

Gruère, G., C. Ashley and J. Cadilhon (2018), "Reforming water policies in agriculture: Lessons from past reforms", *OECD Food, Agriculture and Fisheries Papers*, No. 113, OECD Publishing, Paris, https://dx.doi.org/10.1787/1826beee-en. [6]

Gruère, G. and H. Le Boëdec (2019), "Navigating pathways to reform water policies in agriculture", *OECD Food, Agriculture and Fisheries Papers*, No. 128, OECD Publishing, Paris, https://dx.doi.org/10.1787/906cea2b-en. [13]

Henderson, B. and J. Lankoski (2019), *The environmental impacts of agriculture policies*, OECD Food, Agriculture, and Fisheries Papers No. 130, OECD Publishing, Paris, https://doi.org/10.1787/add0f27c-en. [12]

OECD (2020), *Financing Water Supply, Sanitation and Flood Protection: Challenges in EU Member States and Policy Options*, OECD Studies on Water, OECD Publishing, Paris, https://dx.doi.org/10.1787/6893cdac-en. [1]

OECD (2020), "Nature-based solutions for adapting to water-related climate risks", *OECD Environment Policy Papers*, No. 21, OECD Publishing, Paris, https://dx.doi.org/10.1787/2257873d-en. [18]

OECD (2019), *OECD Environmental Performance Reviews: Australia 2019*, OECD Publishing, http://dx.doi.org/10.1787/9789264310452-en. [20]

OECD (2019), *Innovation, Agricultural Productivity and Sustainability in Japan*, https://doi.org/10.1787/24114278. [2]

OECD (2019), *Making Blended Finance Work for Water and Sanitation: Unlocking Commercial Finance for SDG 6*, OECD Studies on Water, OECD Publishing, Paris, https://dx.doi.org/10.1787/5efc8950-en. [22]

OECD (2019), *OECD Survey on the Implementation of the Recommendation on Water.* [10]

OECD (2019), *Pharmaceutical Residues in Freshwater: Hazards and Policy Responses*, OECD Studies on Water, OECD Publishing, Paris, https://dx.doi.org/10.1787/c936f42d-en. [4]

OECD (2018), *Financing water: Investing in sustainable growth*, OECD Publishing, https://www.oecd.org/water/Policy-Paper-Financing-Water-Investing-in-Sustainable-Growth.pdf. [17]

OECD (2018), *Managing the Water-Energy-Land-Food Nexus in Korea: Policies and Governance Options*, OECD Studies on Water, OECD Publishing, Paris, https://dx.doi.org/10.1787/9789264306523-en. [9]

OECD (2018), *Preventing the Flooding of the Seine in the Paris–Ile de France Region: Progress Made and Future Challenges*, OECD Publishing, Paris, https://dx.doi.org/10.1787/9789264289932-en. [8]

OECD (2017), *Water Charges in Brazil: The Ways Forward*, OECD Studies on Water, OECD Publishing, Paris, https://dx.doi.org/10.1787/9789264285712-en. [11]

OECD (2015), *The Governance of Water Regulators*, OECD Studies on Water, OECD Publishing, Paris, https://dx.doi.org/10.1787/9789264231092-en. [21]

OECD (2015), *Water and Cities: Ensuring Sustainable Futures*, OECD Studies on Water, OECD Publishing, Paris, https://dx.doi.org/10.1787/9789264230149-en. [5]

OECD (2014), *Water Governance in the Netherlands: Fit for the Future?*, OECD Studies on Water, OECD Publishing, Paris, https://dx.doi.org/10.1787/9789264102637-en. [7]

OECD (2012), *A Framework for Financing Water Resources Management*, OECD Publishing, https://doi.org/10.1787/9789264179820-en. [3]

OECD (2012), *Water Quality and Agriculture: Meeting the Policy Challenge*, OECD Studies on Water, OECD Publishing, Paris, https://dx.doi.org/10.1787/9789264168060-en. [14]

OECD (2012), *Water Quality and Agriculture: Meeting the Policy Challenge*, OECD Studies on Water, OECD Publishing, Paris, https://dx.doi.org/10.1787/9789264168060-en. [16]

OECD (2009), *Strategic Financial Planning for Water Supply and Sanitation: A report from the OECD Task Team on Sustainable Financing to Ensure Affordable Access to Water Supply and Sanitation*, OECD Publishing, https://www.oecd.org/env/resources/43949580.pdf. [15]

OECD, FAO, IIASA (2020), *Towards a G20 Action Plan on Water. Background note to the G20 Saudi Presidency*. [19]

Notes

[1] https://www.water.org.uk/wp-content/uploads/2018/11/WaterUK-WRLTPF_Final-Report_FINAL-PUBLISHED-min.pdf

8. Pricing instruments for water management and services

This chapter presents Adherents' experience with pricing instruments for water management and services, in line with the OECD Recommendation on Water. The chapter explores how Adherents set abstractions charges that reflect water scarcity; water pollution charges to incentivise pollution prevention; as well as tariffs that cover operation, maintenance and renewal costs of service provision. It highlights examples of pricing instruments accounting for the redistributive consequences and priority water uses. It also explores efforts to phase out price-distorting policy measures and general subsidies. Finally, the chapter reports valuable efforts to reduce transaction costs when designing pricing instruments.

Adherents to the Recommendation are encouraged to "consider establishing pricing instruments where appropriate and applicable, in combination with other instruments (e.g. regulatory, voluntary or other economic instruments), to manage water resources (in particular water conservation), phase out negative externalities (e.g. overuse, pollution) and improve the financial sustainability of water infrastructures and water services. Economic instruments should reflect each country's social and economic conditions." To that end, the Recommendation suggests "Adherents that consider pricing instruments to take a number of considerations into account":

The use of economic policy instruments discussed hereafter are often combined with other instruments (e.g. regulation, information, voluntary approaches) to manage water quantity, such as water allocation regimes (section 3) and to manage water quality, such as through effluent standards (section 4).

Agriculture specificities are mentioned throughout this section, as this is an area where Adherents' policies are less aligned to the Recommendation than with other sections, despite the importance of the sector in water use and pollution. Acknowledging that misalignment may be due to preferences not to use pricing instruments, Figure 8.1 estimated average alignment indices in 2009 and 2019 for section 8.

Figure 8.1. Average alignment of agriculture and water policies with section 8 of the Recommendation on Water

Changes from 2009 to 2019. Alignment indices range from zero to one. Higher indices indicate a better alignment.

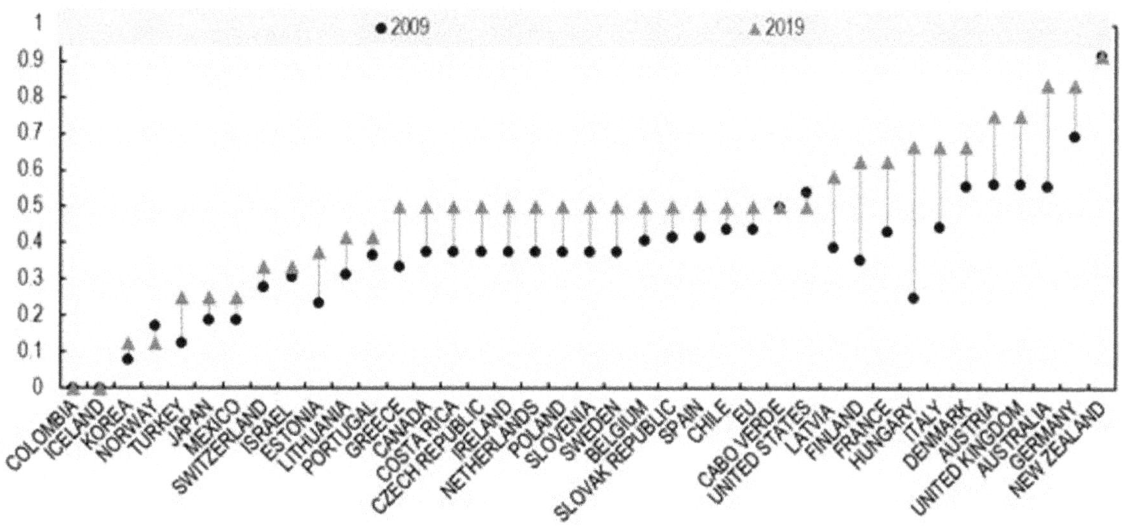

Note: The index was adjusted to account for the fact that countries' possible preferences not to use pricing.
Source: (Gruère, Shigemitsu and Crawford, 2020[1])

8.1. Setting abstraction charges that reflect water scarcity

Adherents to the Recommendation that are considering pricing instruments would benefit from "setting abstraction charges for surface and ground water that reflect water scarcity (i.e. environmental and resource cost) and that cover administrative costs of managing the system".

The 2019 OECD Implementation Survey shows abstraction charges for groundwater exist that in 74 % of respondents, 74% for surface water. Abstraction charges for groundwater often apply to industrial users (in 59 % of respondents), and slightly less frequently - in 44% of respondents - to domestic uses. For surface water, abstraction charges are most frequently applied to energy producers (in 63 % of respondents) (Table 8.1). In agriculture, 17 of 38 surveyed adherents on water and agriculture policy changes reported that they used pricing as an instrument to manage water demand, which represents a low rate but in significant progression since 2009. More detailed reviews are required to decipher whether abstraction charges are designed to signal the opportunity cost of water (as water policy instruments) or to generate a revenue (as a financing instrument).

Table 8.1. The use of abstraction charges for ground and surface water

	Groundwater					Surface water			
	Agriculture	Domestic	Industrial	Energy Production	Other	Agriculture	Industrial	Energy Production	Other
Austria	n/a	n/a	n/a	n/a	n/a	n/a	n/a	n/a	n/a
Canada			•				•		
Chile	n/a	n/a	n/a	n/a	n/a	n/a	n/a	n/a	n/a
Czech Republic	•	•	•	•		•	•	•	
Estonia		•	•	•		•	•	•	
Finland	n/a	n/a	n/a	n/a	n/a	n/a	n/a	n/a	n/a
France	•	•	•	•		•	•	•	•
Hungary	•		•	•	•	•	•	•	•
Ireland	n/a	n/a	n/a	n/a	n/a	n/a	n/a	n/a	n/a
Israel	•						•		
Italy	•	•	•	•	•	•	•	•	•
Japan					•	n/a	n/a	n/a	n/a
Korea			•			•	•	•	•
Latvia	•	•	•			•	•	•	
Lithuania	•	•	•	•	•	•	•	•	
Luxemburg	•	•	•	•	•	•	•	•	•
Mexico		•	•	•	•		•	•	•
Netherlands	•		•		•				
Norway	n/a	n/a	n/a	n/a	n/a			•	
Portugal	•	•	•			•	•	•	•
Slovak Republic	•		•	•	•	•	•	•	•
Spain	•	•	•	•		•	•	•	
Sweden	n/a	n/a	n/a	n/a	n/a	n/a	n/a	n/a	n/a
Turkey	•					•	•	•	
United Kingdom	•	•	•	•		•	•	•	
United States	n/a	n/a	n/a	n/a	n/a				•
Costa Rica	•	•	•		•	•	•	•	

Note: This table is based on the responses to the *Part 2 – Financing for water management* section of the questionnaire. n/a is applied for countries which answered "no" to the questions "Do abstraction charges for groundwater/surface exist in your country?".
Source: Authors, based on the 2019 OECD Survey on the Implementation of the OECD Council Recommendation on Water.

Abstraction charges for both surface and underground water are absent in only three responding Adherents, namely **Austria**, **Chile** and **Sweden**. **Austria** and **Sweden** are water-abundant Adherents, which may explain the situation. **Chile** extensively relies on market instruments to allocate water where it is most needed.

Most abstraction charges are based on the price per volume of water abstracted, with the user paying a unitary rate per cubic meter abstracted or using a two tier tariff system (fixed charge and volumetric above some level). Some charges are also fixed per hectare for agricultural abstraction, a price per megawatt-hour for energy production or nominal license fees linked to an abstraction permit regime (see section Water allocation regimes) like in the **United Kingdom** (Gruère, Shigemitsu and Crawford, 2020[1]). Water abstraction charges are commonly managed at the sub-national level. For instance, they are set at the regional level in **Belgium**, provincial level in **Canada**, and at state level (Land) in **Germany**, at the hydrographic basin level in **France** (with a legislated national price ceiling) and by four devolved administrations in the **United Kingdom** (OECD, 2017[2]).

To reflect the geographical and temporal variations in water scarcity levels, water abstraction charges can be flexibly adapted. In **France**, the threshold under which water users are exempt from paying abstraction charges depends on the water agency, the type of resource and the scarcity of water (OECD, 2017[2]). In **Portugal**, a legislated scarcity coefficient for different river basins is being used to reflect different levels of water scarcity geographically and temporarily throughout the year (OECD, 2015[3]). Spatial and seasonal variation can be particularly important in agriculture, it was used in some ways by 30% of the Adherents responding to the survey of water and agriculture policies. For instance, in **Greece**, water pricing is differentiated by region, while in **Hungary**, pressure multipliers are applied to raise prices in groundwater bodies facing water risks.[1]

In contrast, many water abstraction charges do not differentiate varying levels of water availability. The 2015 OECD Survey of Water Resources Allocation found that abstraction charges generally do not reflect water scarcity or the opportunity cost of using water. In those cases, the costs of depleting water levels is borne by the community at large rather than targeting those that use more water during scarce times or in scarce regions. In periods of severe scarcity, pricing instruments are usually supplemented by regulatory instruments restricting certain usages, such as in **France** or **Japan** where restrictions on low-value water uses are implemented during periods of scarcity (e.g. ban on washing cars, gardening or filling in private swimming pools).

Figure 8.2. Reflecting water scarcity in water charges

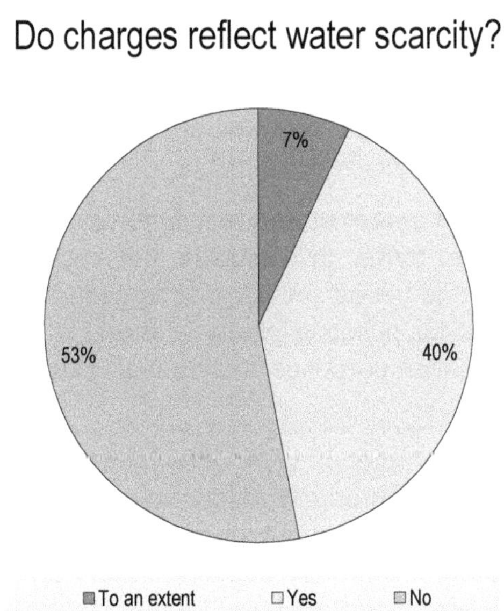

Source: Based on the country profiles of 27 OECD and key partner countries available here: http://www.oecd.org/fr/publications/water-resources-allocation-9789264229631-en.htm

The level of the water charge is usually different based on whether it is sourced from groundwater or surface water. Some Adherents, federal states or water basins apply unique water charge to all types of sources (**France** (Seine-Normandy), **Germany** (13 of 16 federal states) (Gruère, Shigemitsu and

Crawford, 2020[1]). Special zones, aquifer, or rivers are subject to specific rates (e.g. Water Distribution Areas in **France** or specific aquifers in the Flemish region in **Belgium** and in **Estonia**). Higher charges are often imposed on groundwater than on surface water (one exception is the **Czech Republic**) (OECD, 2017[4]).

Adherents usually differentiate the rate of abstraction charges by the type of users (e.g. agriculture, domestic, industrial, energy production). This imperfectly reflects the pressure on the resource. For instance, water used to cool thermal plants is usually returned to the river body (albeit at a higher temperature). The agricultural sector commonly benefits from lower rates or from exemptions, so does the use of potable water, such as in Flanders (Belgium) (OECD, 2017[4]).

The objective of employing abstraction charges is not always explicitly stated. However, in Baden-Württemberg, **Germany**, and in **Brazil**, the use of water abstraction charges is to incentive users to save water. In **Belgium**, **France**, **Hungary** and the **Netherlands** abstraction charge proceeds are used for environmental protection. In some cases, very specific objectives are being pursued, such as in the **Netherlands** where revenues from abstraction charges are used to finance groundwater depletion research.

8.2. Setting water pollution charges to incentivise pollution prevention

Adherents to the recommendation that are considering pricing instruments would benefit from "setting water pollution charges for surface and groundwater use and pollution or charges for wastewater discharge at a sufficient level to have a significant incentive effect to prevent and control pollution."

15 out of 26 Adherents responding to the 2019 OECD Implementation Survey have an effluent discharge tax (Table 8.2). They are levied based on either the volume discharged only, proportion exceeding a certain threshold, or also based on the effluent's pollution content (related for instance to the oxygen demand and suspended solids, nutrients, heavy metals and persistent chemicals). **Colombia** taxes discharge of total suspended solids and BOD (OECD, 2019[5]). The high level of emissions taxes set in the **Netherlands** in the 1970s helped drastically reduce total organic emissions and industrial organic emissions. Similarly, high emissions taxes have been implemented in **Germany**, the **Czech Republic** (ground and surface water), and **Slovenia**, in order to encourage behavioural change and reduce water pollution (OECD, 2017[6]).

Wastewater charges exist in most **EU member states** (e.g. Estonia, France, Italy, Netherlands and Spain). They also exist elsewhere in different forms. In **Australia**, there are fees for some water pollutants in certain catchments and charges on land-based sewage discharge in the Great Barrier Reef area. (OECD, 2019[5]). An additional tariff was set for polluting plants in **Israel** to ensure that the effluent quality is sufficiently high to be reused for irrigation purposes. Only a few, mostly EU member states, report using water pollution charges in agriculture.

Levying charges on diffuse water pollution tends to be done by using approximations for example based on acreage, number of cattle, or by taxing products responsible for the pollution (e.g. tax on fertiliser and other agricultural chemicals). A dozen Adherents put an additional price on pesticide use either through a tax, a duty or a control fee (**Australia** (Australian Capital Territory and New South Wales)[2], **Denmark, Finland, France, Italy, Mexico, Norway** and **Sweden**) (Table 8.2). Florida (**United States**) taxes imports of pollutants including pesticides. On the other hand, **Belgium** (Flanders) provides subsidies for the reduction of pesticide and fertiliser use in ornamental crops cultivation (OECD, 2019[5]).

Table 8.2. Examples of features of pollution charges in selected Adherents

Examples

Country	Levied by	Tax name	Specific tax	Tax structure
Australia	State	Water effluent charge	Volume, pollution content (types of polluants)	Per kg assessable load
Canada	Province	Charge on discharge	Volume and pollution content	Per litre or per tonne
Denmark		Diffuse source	Chemical deterrents of insects and mammals	Tax on retail price
France		Diffuse source	Pesticides	Per kg
		Water effluent charges	Households	Per m^3
Netherlands		Tax on the pollution of surface waters	BOD, COD and heavy metals, for large polluters	Per pollution unit
Sweden	Municipality	Wastewater user charges	Wastewater and drinking water	Varies by municipality; full cost charging
		Diffuse source	Pesticides	Per whole kg active constituent

Source: (OECD, 2017[7]) using the OECD database on Policy Instruments for the Environment (accessed 20/03/2016)

In some cases, downstream beneficiaries pay to regulate or preserve or restore upstream environments (e.g. flood management), as they benefit from activities made by others to reduce water consumption or pollution (i.e. payments for ecosystem services). Upstream land and water users/polluters receive compensation to provide environmental services and avoid damaging practices: in Korea users downstream of the 4 rivers compensate users upstream for constraints in abstracting and using water (OECD, 2017[4]).

8.3. Setting tariffs that cover operation, maintenance and renewal costs

Adherents to the recommendation that are considering pricing instruments would benefit from "setting tariffs or charges for water services and all other uses that cover the operation, maintenance and renewal costs of infrastructure and a progressive proportion of capital costs, where possible."

The principle of "full cost recovery" as enshrined in article 9 of the **EU** WFD provides for water supply and sanitation tariffs to cover the costs of water supply and sanitation, including operation and capital costs as well as environmental and resource costs associated with the consumption of the service (OECD, 2010[8]). More recently, sustainable cost recovery has been considered a practical and fair combination of user charges and public transfers, which requires that tariffs are affordable for each category of users and transfers are predictable, enabling the water utility to count on them to finance investment (OECD, 2010[8]).

Cost recovery is particularly low in the agriculture sector; irrigating farmers do not generally pay for the cost of water they can access. Despite progress since 2009, only nine of 39 survey respondents have full cost recovery related to both capital cost and operations and maintenance for irrigation, most of which do not have large irrigation areas (Table 8.3). In **Germany**, operation and maintenance as well as capital costs for abstraction are borne fully by operators and the federal states set different abstraction fees, some of which internalise parts of the environment and resource costs. In most cases, Adherents partially recover operation and maintenance costs and/or capital costs. For instance, cost recovery is low in the **Mexican** agricultural sector and there is no full recovery of costs related to capital cost and operations and maintenance for irrigation. Cost recovery is even less common for groundwater, although the situation differs from surface water as costs are often borne by users of individual wells.

Table 8.3. Water cost recovery in agriculture

2019

		Operations and maintenance cost recovery	
		Less than 100%	100%
Capital cost recovery	Less than 100%	Chile, Korea, Mexico, Norway, Portugal, Spain, Switzerland	Costa Rica, France[3], Italy, Japan, United States
	100%	Australia, Turkey	Austria, Denmark, Estonia, Finland, Germany, Israel, New Zealand, Sweden, United Kingdom

Notes: The cost recovery had not been assessed in Lithuania. Cabo Verde does not license surface water. No responses were given by Belgium, Colombia, Czech Republic, Iceland, and Latvia. The EU requires full cost recovery under the Water Framework Directive.
Source: (Gruère, Shigemitsu and Crawford, 2020[1])

The structure and level of tariffs and charges, which help to ensure the delivery of water services to households and businesses, varies among and within Adherents. They are usually composed of a fixed charge, which covers connection costs to the public water supply and/or sewage systems, and a volumetric rating system (if metering is available), which covers the volume of water supplied. Different tariff structures and levels will have differentiated social impacts (Leflaive and Hjort, 2020[9]). In **Australia**, water prices paid users reflect the cost of service provision and the volumes of water used, and also reflect the costs associated with natural resource management. They vary according to geographical circumstances, depending on whether the services are urban (treated water) or rural (untreated water) and the level of adherence to economic pricing principles.

The level of financial cost recovery varies from one Adherent to another – with the caveat that a full picture of how tariffs and charges cover costs of service provision is still lacking. Indeed, many OECD Adherents do not provide sufficient transparency on costs (e.g. deferred maintenance and replacements) or subsidies provided to fill the gap between the costs and revenues, making the estimation of cost recovery difficult (OECD, 2009[10]). In **New Zealand**, water charges recover costs associated with consent administration, information gathering and monitoring/supervision.

A limited number of Adherents manage to cover a progressive proportion of capital costs of infrastructure, in addition to their operation and maintenance costs. This is the case in **Austria, Denmark, Finland, New Zealand, Sweden** and the **United Kingdom.**

In cases where the water infrastructure costs are not covered by revenues raised through tariffs and charges, Adherents provide subsidies to fill the gap. This is the case in **Spain** where new wastewater treatment plants are partly subsidised by the EU and the central government. In **France**, the proceeds of water-related charges are recycled to subsidise investments in water services (most particularly wastewater treatment plants) at basin level.

8.4. Accounting for the redistributive consequences and priority water uses

The Adherents to the Recommendation that are considering pricing instruments should "account for redistributive consequences and priority water uses, based on affordability studies, equity for vulnerable groups and assessment of competitiveness impacts, as appropriate, taking into account the right to safe drinking water and sanitation."

The 2019 OECD Implementation Survey revealed that 89% of respondents have measures to address affordability issues for water and sanitation services for low-income households in place (Figure 8.3). The mechanisms to address affordability issues are varied, though most Adherents seem to use reduced water and sanitation tariffs for households with low revenues (Figure 8.4).

Figure 8.3. Mechanisms to address affordability issues for water and sanitation services for low-income households

Note: Responses to the question "Does your country have mechanisms to address affordability issues for water and sanitation services for low income households?".
Source: 2019 survey on the implementation of the OECD Council Recommendation on Water; 27 responses received, including 26 Adherents.

Figure 8.4. Mechanisms to address affordability issues

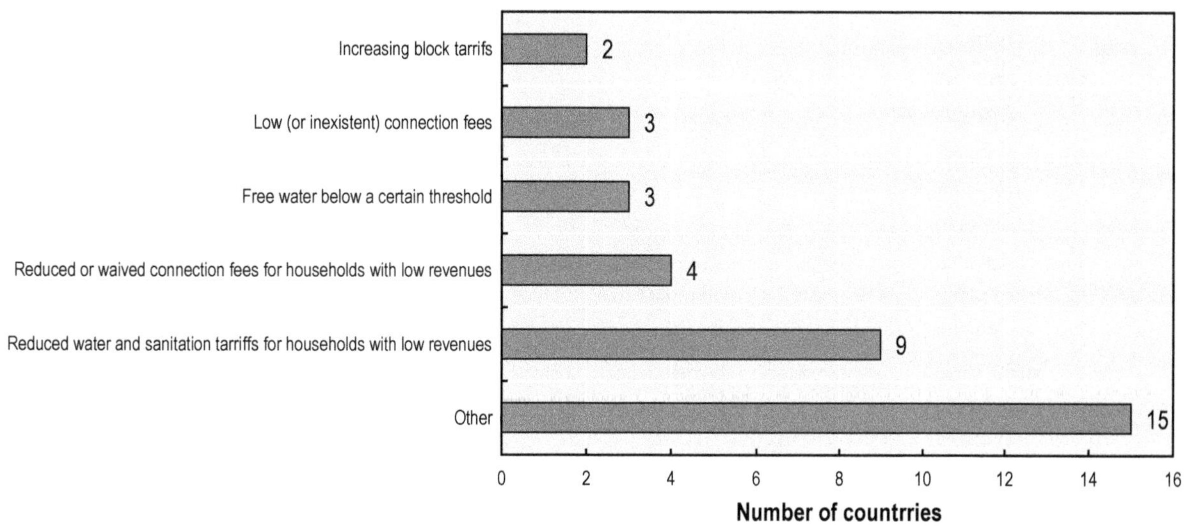

Note: Responses to the question: "How is support for low income households provided?". "Other" includes: plans from water supply companies, solutions provided on the local and municipal level and the aid via welfare system. Multiple responses were possible. Excludes responses from Latvia, Slovak Republic and Sweden.
Source: 2019 survey on the implementation of the OECD Council Recommendation on Water; 27 responses received, including 26 Adherents.

In **Chile**, targeted subsidies, which are fully funded by the central government and administered by the municipalities, support low-income households for whom the water supply and sanitation bill constitutes more than 5% of their monthly income. The subsidy covers between 25 to 85 % of their basic water and sewerage consumption (up to a certain level). In 2011, 15% of water company clients benefited from this subsidy at a cost of USD 80 million (Leflaive and Hjort, 2020[9]). In selected **French** cities (e.g. through the suburban *Syndicat des eaux d'Ile-de-France*) rebates, vouchers or lump sum transfers are provided to pay for water bills for eligible water users under the Programme "Aide Eau Solidaire" (Leflaive and Hjort, 2020[9]). In **Australia**, residential customers may access financial hardship assistance programmes provided by water utilities, which include flexible payment options, not restricting supply and deferral of debt collection for customers receiving assistance.

A study on water affordability (Figure 8.5) indicates that a vast majority of water users could afford to pay more for water supply and sanitation services. This suggests that cheap water (or tariffs that do not provide the revenues to cover operation, maintenance and renewal costs) benefit people who do not need such support, and potentially affects poor population (who are more vulnerable to low-level of service).

Figure 8.5. Share of water supply and sanitation expenditures in households' disposable income

Percentage, 2011-2015 average

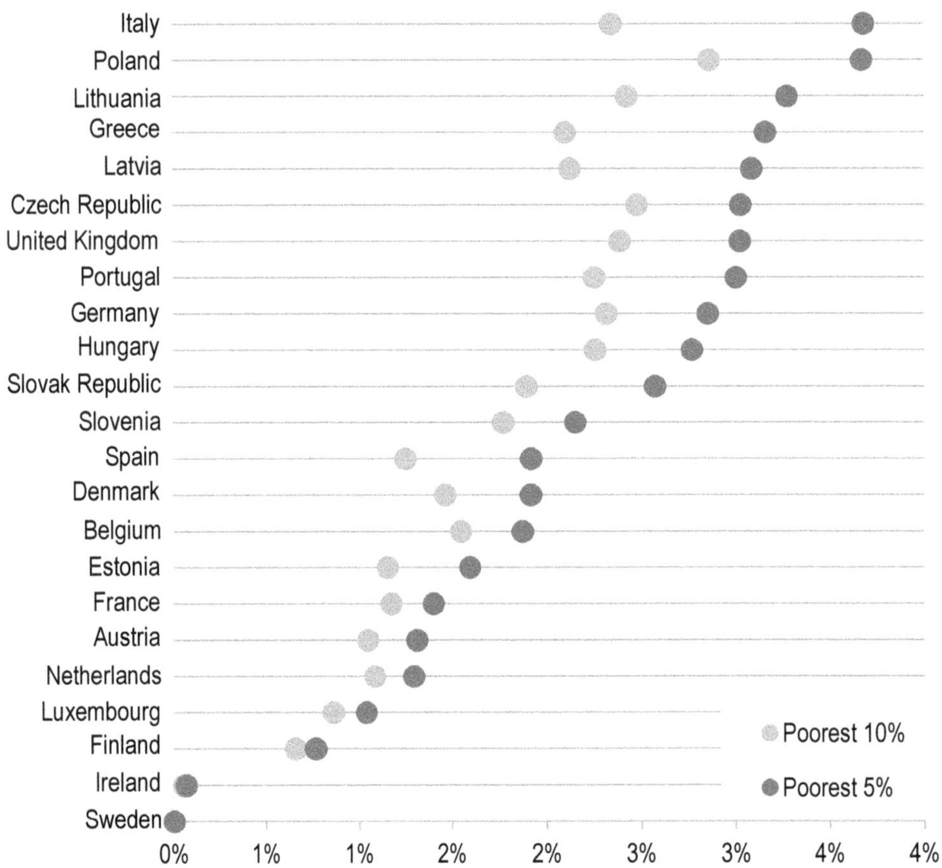

Note: Lack of household expenditure data for Sweden.
Source: (OECD, 2020[11]); based on EUROSTAT (household expenditures and income data).

In **Portugal**, the economic regulator of water supply and sanitation services carried out an affordability study to identify geographically concentrated clusters of population that would fall above the affordability threshold as part of the design of its proposed tariff reform (Leflaive and Hjort, 2020[9]). It showed that about 10.5% of Portuguese households had bills above the affordability criteria, concentrated in 60 out of 309 municipalities in the North and Tagus Valley regions. The tariff reform allows flexible solutions in different municipalities.

Box 8.1. Denmark's experience in considering price elasticity of water demand

Denmark has a long tradition for water consumption metering and consumer charges for water supply and waste water treatment. Since 1992, urban WSS tariffs in Denmark have been based on full recovery of economic and environmental costs. During the period 1993-2004, water prices increased by 54%, leading to a decrease in urban water demand from 155 to 125 litres per person per day. In 2015, average consumption per capita was as low as 106 litres per day.

The average Danish family now pays 1.6% of their annual income in WSS charges. From the water bill paid by consumers, approximately 50% goes to the wastewater companies, 30% to the government and close to 20% to drinking water utilities.

A strong guiding principle for the financing of WSS services in Denmark is that supply policy and social policy should not be mixed. Thus, there is no social tariff, and affordability of water and waste water services is ensured via income support through Danish social policy.

Source: (Leflaive and Hjort, 2020[9])

8.5. Phasing out price-distorting policy measures and general subsidies

Adherents to the recommendation "that are considering pricing instruments would benefit from phasing out price-distorting policy measures and general subsidies that affect water availability, quality and demand, to the extent possible, taking into account broader public policies and priorities."

A range of measures and subsidies contribute to financing water and the management of water resources. Their impact on water demand and availability should be assessed, as some, under certain conditions, can have harmful impact on water availability, quality and demand (Table 8.4).

Table 8.4. Examples of subsidies in water services and water resources management

Transfer mechanism	Example
Direct transfers of funds	Capital investment subsidies for water supply and sanitation providers
Foregone tax revenue	Environmental pollution charges that do not cover the cost of pollution, as well as special reductions or exemptions
Foregone user charge revenue	Water supply and sanitation tariffs that do not cover the cost of service provision; lack of abstraction charges; reduced electricity tariffs for irrigation pumps
Transfer of risk to government	Government compensation to households and firms for property damage due to water-related disasters
Induced transfers	Cross-subsidies for water supply and sanitation services (industrial vs. household tariffs)
Economic advantage due to unequal regulation or policy	Different regulations or charges for industry discharging pollutants to sewer systems or directly to water bodies

Note: This is not an exhaustive list.
Source: adapted from (EAP Task Force, 2013[12]).

Sectoral policies can play an important role in incentivising water use. This is the case of agriculture, a sector that is still subject to high level of support in Adherents, with producer support estimates amounting to 18.5% of gross farm receipt or USD 235 billion/year in 2016-18 (OECD, 2019[13]). Certain type of agricultural support that encourages input use or production without environmental or resource constraints directly or indirectly via measures inflating prices, can impact water quality and water quantity, among other environmental impacts (Henderson and Lankoski, 2019[14]) (DeBoe, 2020[15]) (Gruère and Le Boëdec, 2019[16]) (OECD, 2020[17]).

This includes subsidies for inputs like fertilizers without constraints, but also subsidies encouraging the production of specific commodities and most importantly a wide range of measures that inflate producer prices for specific commodities higher than necessary. Supporting certain production type will encourage farmers to stay in production regardless of water conditions, and of environmental impacts. As shown in Figure 8.6, even if this type of support - identified as potentially most distorting measures - were reduced significantly the past twenty years, it still represents a large share of agriculture support in a number of OECD Adherents. At the same time, governments support directly for irrigation (Figure 8.7), which may or may not harm water, has been declining significantly in Adherents (Gruère and Le Boëdec, 2019[16]).

Figure 8.6. Agriculture support in percentage of gross farm receipts

By country, share of gross farm receipts, 2017-19

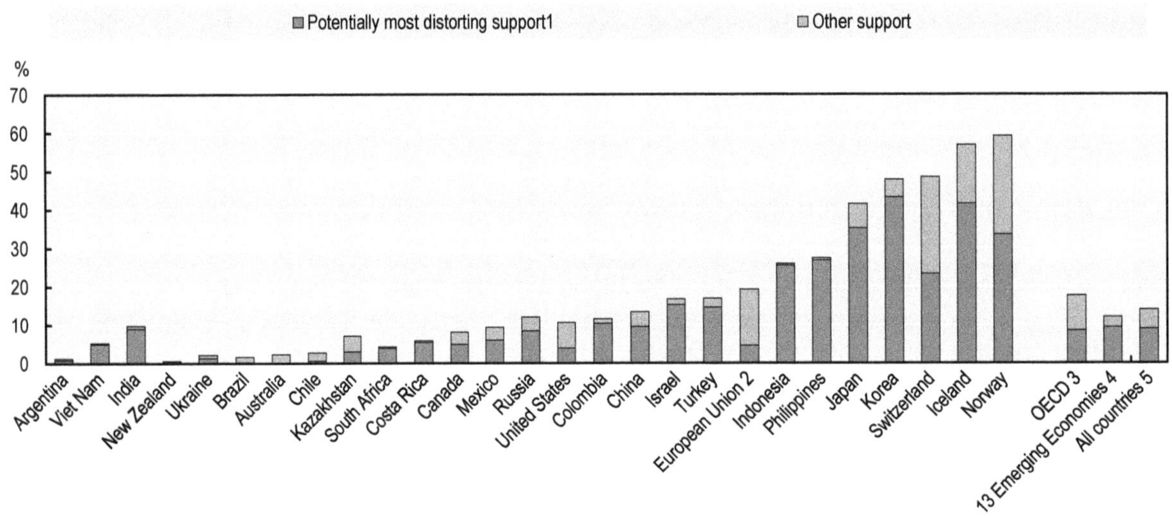

Notes: Countries are ranked according to the %PSE levels. Negative market price support is not shown. 1) Positive market price support, support based on output payments and on the unconstrained use of variable inputs. 2) EU28. 3) The OECD total does not include the non-OECD EU Member States. 4) The 13 Emerging Economies include Argentina, Brazil, China, Colombia (now an OECD member), Costa Rica, India, Indonesia, Kazakhstan, the Philippines, Russian Federation, South Africa, Ukraine and Viet Nam. 5) The All countries total includes all OECD countries, non-OECD EU Member States, and the Emerging Economies.

Source: OECD (2020), "Producer and Consumer Support Estimates", OECD Agriculture statistics (database), http://dx.doi.org/10.1787/agr-pcse-data-en in (OECD, 2020[17]).

Figure 8.7. Irrigation related producer support estimates (1986-2016)

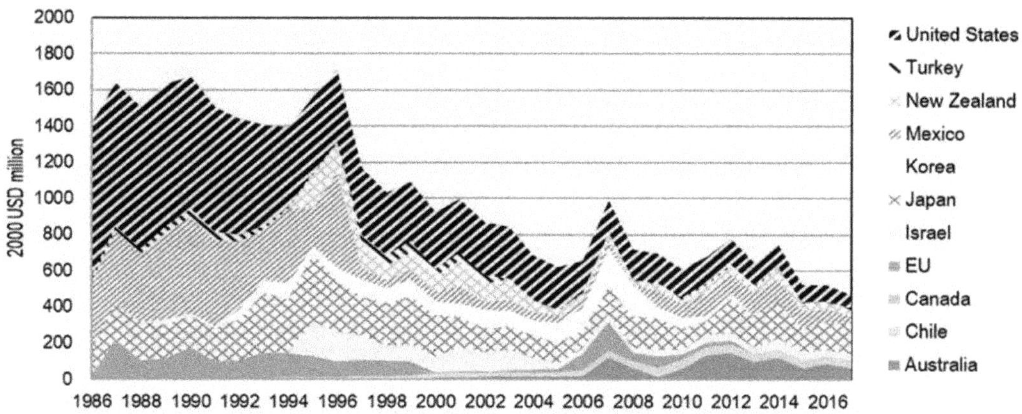

Note: Countries without support for irrigation are excluded.
Source: OECD (2019), "Producer and Consumer Support Estimates", OECD Agriculture statistics (database), http://dx.doi.org/10.1787/agr-pcse-data-en.

8.6. Transaction costs

Adherents to the Recommendation "that are considering pricing instruments would benefit from considering transaction costs, including administrative costs, when designing pricing instruments and revenue management schemes."

Different pricing instruments for water management services will generate a range of transaction costs to estimate, implement, administer and levy the instrument. These costs can be disproportionate to the benefit expected from the instrument.

This is clearly illustrated by discussions on the costs and benefits of metering household consumption for water tariffs. (Reynaud et al., 2016[18]) state that while domestic users commonly are found to be sensitive to prices, the elasticity of water use to price changes is, in most cases, relatively small. As a consequence, in absence of significant tariff increases, metering household water consumption will generally not affect water uses and water bills. Meters can still be used to detect leakage, and this can be done through block or district metering. Metering at household level can be disproportionately costly to support sophisticated tariff structures, which have little impact on water use (Leflaive and Hjort, 2020[9]). Such a discussion was particularly vibrant in **Ireland** when Irish Water endeavoured to roll out systematic metering at household level in the context of a reform of financing strategy for water supply and sanitation services.

Similar discussions apply to the design of responses to affordability issues. The most appropriate responses usually combine a capacity to target households most in need of support; synergies with water conservation measures; and low transaction costs, building on existing data and social programmes. More detailed analyses are required to document how Adherent consider (and minimise) transaction costs when designing water pricing schemes and related measures to address affordability issues.

New sources of data, digitalisation and other technologies can reduce transaction costs. Under the National Water Initiative, **Australia** is pursuing to minimise transaction costs on water trades, including through good information flows in the market and compatible entitlement, registry, regulatory and other arrangements across jurisdictions (OECD, 2019[19]).

References

DeBoe, G. (2020), "Impacts of agricultural policies on productivity and sustainability performance in agriculture: A literature review", *OECD Food, Agriculture and Fisheries Papers*, No. 141, OECD Publishing, Paris, https://dx.doi.org/10.1787/6bc916e7-en. [15]

EAP Task Force (2013), *Improving the Use of Economic Instruments for Water Resource Management in Kyrgyzstan: The Case of Lake Issyk-Kul Basin*, OECD Publishing, https://www.oecd.org/env/outreach/2013_Kyrgyz%20report%20on%20Eis%20for%20WRM%20Eng%20Web.pdf. [12]

Gruère, G. and H. Le Boëdec (2019), "Navigating pathways to reform water policies in agriculture", *OECD Food, Agriculture and Fisheries Papers*, No. 128, OECD Publishing, Paris, https://dx.doi.org/10.1787/906cea2b-en. [16]

Gruère, G., M. Shigemitsu and S. Crawford (2020), "Agriculture and water policy changes: Stocktaking and alignment with OECD and G20 recommendations", *OECD Food, Agriculture and Fisheries Papers*, No. 144, OECD Publishing, Paris, https://dx.doi.org/10.1787/f35e64af-en. [1]

Henderson, B. and J. Lankoski (2019), *The environmental impacts of agriculture policies*, OECD Food, Agriculture, and Fisheries Papers No. 130, OECD Publishing, Paris, https://doi.org/10.1787/add0f27c-en. [14]

Leflaive, X. and M. Hjort (2020), "Addressing the social consequences of tariffs for water supply and sanitation", *OECD Environment Working Papers*, No. 166, OECD Publishing, Paris, https://dx.doi.org/10.1787/afede7d6-en. [9]

OECD (2020), *Agricultural Policy Monitoring and Evaluation 2020*, OECD Publishing, Paris, https://dx.doi.org/10.1787/928181a8-en. [17]

OECD (2020), *Financing Water Supply, Sanitation and Flood Protection: Challenges in EU Member States and Policy Options*, OECD Studies on Water, OECD Publishing, Paris, https://dx.doi.org/10.1787/6893cdac-en. [11]

OECD (2019), *OECD Environmental Performance Reviews: Australia 2019*, OECD Publishing, http://dx.doi.org/10.1787/9789264310452-en. [19]

OECD (2019), *Agricultural Policy Monitoring and Evaluation 2019*, OECD Publishing, Paris, http://dx.doi.org/10.1787/39bfe6f3-en. [13]

OECD (2019), "Policy Instruments for the Environment (PINE)", *OECD Statistics (database)*, http://oe.cd/pine (accessed on 9 October 2019). [5]

OECD (2017), *Diffuse Pollution, Degraded Waters: Emerging Policy Solutions*, OECD Studies on Water, OECD Publishing, Paris, https://dx.doi.org/10.1787/9789264269064-en. [7]

OECD (2017), *Enhancing Water Use Efficiency in Korea: Policy Issues and Recommendations*, OECD Studies on Water, OECD Publishing, Paris, https://dx.doi.org/10.1787/9789264281707-en. [4]

OECD (2017), *Enhancing Water Use Efficiency in Korea: Policy Issues and Recommendations*, OECD Studies on Water, OECD Publishing, Paris, https://dx.doi.org/10.1787/9789264281707-en. [6]

OECD (2017), *Water Charges in Brazil: The Ways Forward*, OECD Studies on Water, OECD Publishing, Paris, https://dx.doi.org/10.1787/9789264285712-en. [2]

OECD (2015), *Water Resources Allocation: Sharing Risks and Opportunities*, OECD Studies on Water, OECD Publishing, Paris, https://dx.doi.org/10.1787/9789264229631-en. [3]

OECD (2010), *Pricing Water Resources and Water and Sanitation Services*, OECD Studies on Water, OECD Publishing, Paris, https://dx.doi.org/10.1787/9789264083608-en. [8]

OECD (2009), *Strategic Financial Planning for Water Supply and Sanitation: A report from the OECD Task Team on Sustainable Financing to Ensure Affordable Access to Water Supply and Sanitation*, OECD Publishing, https://www.oecd.org/env/resources/43949580.pdf. [10]

Reynaud, A. et al. (2016), *Review on International Best Practices on Charges for Water Management*, Toulouse School of Economics. [18]

Notes

[1] 2019 OECD Survey on water and agriculture policy changes (Gruère, Shigemitsu and Crawford, 2020[1])

[2] Australian Capital Territory: Pesticides and Polychlorinated biphenyls (PCBs) emissions to water from sewage treatment plants -- more than 10,000 ML per year + New South Wales: Pesticide and PCB emissions to water

[3] Full cost recovery for agricultural use in France, including environmental costs (overseas departments included) is estimated to more than 60%. This low level is mainly explained by the estimated amount linked to environmental degradation compensated by other water users or not compensated altogether. Without taking into account environmental costs, this recovery rate goes back to 90% (this result includes the cost of collective services, private costs and financial transfers between the different categories of users). This estimate made in 2019 is the first to have been conducted both at the basin level and at the national level.

www.ingramcontent.com/pod-product-compliance
Ingram Content Group UK Ltd.
Pitfield, Milton Keynes, MK11 3LW, UK
UKHW051240300926
15471UKWH00015B/1445

9 789264 653597